PIRATE GOSPEL

EDDIE JONES

DRY BONES PUBLISHING

PIRATE GOSPEL: SET SAIL WITH JESUS, MATE by Eddie Jones™

Published by Dry Bones Publishing

Jones, Eddie, 1957–

Pirate Gospel: Set Sail with Jesus, Mate / by Eddie Jones. 1st ed. p. cm.
Summary: [Publisher to insert summary here]

ISBN: 978-1-965649-25-1

Cover design by Skip Lively

Interior design by atritex.com

Available in print from your local bookstore, online, or from the publisher.

For more information on this book and the author visit:
www.pirate-gospel.com

Printed in the United States of America

Chapter One

Your Abundant Life in Paradise

René Duguay-Trouin were no lubber by birthright with noble connections. He were a sailor's sailor — born in the port city of St Malo, France, in 1673, drawn to the sea the way iron is drawn to a lodestone, and capable of making English naval commanders grip the rails of their own vessels and stare at the horizon in the manner of men who had recently eaten something that disagreed with them.

> *"Ye were made for abundant life — the kind that enjoys time, passages, and people, yes, but also enjoys sharing the blessings of Skipper."*

He joined the French Navy at sixteen. By eighteen, he had his first command. By twenty-one, he had clapped eyes on the deck of the powerful forty-gun *Hermine* and made her his own. The English and Dutch gave him a wide berth — or paid the price when they didn't. Prize after prize struck their colours before him. Hand over fist, he built a fortune and a fearsome reputation in the English Channel and across the Atlantic.

Then, in 1694, the English caught him. Captured, he sat in an English prison, his vessel gone, his freedom gone, his future looking as dark as Davy Jones' Locker.

But Duguay-Trouin were no lily-livered swab. He escaped. The English, who had personally constructed what they described in their own official documents as an escape-proof prison, responded to this development by standing in the empty cell for a long moment and then shrugging. When he made port back in France, he didn't slink in like a bilge rat. He were presented to King Louis XIV himself.

What followed were not a patched-up, hobbled return to the sea. It were a full refit. In 1711, he launched an eleven-day bombardment of Rio de Janeiro — a city that every lubber, naval officer, military strategist, and person who had ever unrolled a map in a professional capacity had declared completely, structurally, and on-their-mother's-grave impregnable.

City officials paid Duguay-Trouin a large pile of money to sail away and leave them alone.

He died an admiral, ennobled, celebrated, and victorious — standing at the exact spot on the map where the English had drawn a large X labeled "Do not let this man go." That's the long and short of it.

Blimey — and that's where René Duguay-Trouin's life crosses our bow. Before time, back when Paradise were in the offing, Skipper built something breathtaking.

Picture a world untouched by pain, where every need be met, every desire be satisfied, and the presence of Skipper be as natural as breathing. No taxes. No bilge duty. No one be playing the lute badly at two in the morning. This were Eden — not merely a garden, but a declaration of what Skipper intended for humanity: abundant life, full and free. Ye might say it were the perfect port — a place to sail from and explore the world.

Into this world, Skipper placed a man. He had everything — land, purpose, dominion, the blessing of his Creator. But Skipper, who knows us better than we know ourselves, saw something missing. So while the man slept, Skipper fashioned a companion from his very side. When the man woke and clapped eyes on her for the first time, his words tumbled out with wonder: *"This is bone of my bones and flesh of my flesh."* (Genesis 2:23)

They were made for each other, and made for a life of partnership with Skipper. Ruling over creation with wisdom and joy, they enjoyed everything Skipper gave 'em.

But within this port be a knave — a scurvy dog — and this be where the treachery of this story starts.

When Every Vessel Starts Taking on Water

The enemy didn't arrive with a cutlass and pistol. He snuck into the boatyard quietly, with questions designed to plant doubt in the sturdiness of our vessel and the wisdom of the Shipwright. He were a loose cannon, that one — whispering to Eve, twisting Skipper's words just enough to make disobedience sound reasonable — even enlightened. And Eve, seduced by the promise of sailing solo without need for charts, compass, or companions, cast off. But Adam, seeing Eve about to depart without him, ran up, latched hold of her hand, and the pair sailed to the great unknown with the knowledge of good, yes, but also wickedness.

In short, they became pirates. And pirating always gives way to that sinking feeling that eventually, the crew will go down to a watery grave.

Sin entered the world, and with it came shame, fear, and separation from Skipper. When Skipper came looking for them, they hid. *"I was afraid,"* Adam confessed, *"because I was naked."* (Genesis 3:10) The intimacy they had known with their Creator were broken. The paradise they had been given were lost.

And because of their corrupted state, they were sent out from the garden, cast out of the Port of Paradise — not in anger, but in love. Skipper had a plan to rescue the pair, but it would take time, require His Son, and cost both a great deal.

Even in judgment, Skipper made provision. He clothed them. He promised that one day, through the offspring of the woman, that knave who roams about making pirates of men and women would be crushed. (Genesis 3:15) The plan of redemption were already in motion before the wreckage of that day had even settled onto the ocean floor.

Though they had gone rogue, Adam and Eve did not lose everything. The authority Skipper granted them over the earth remained. The mandate to be fruitful, multiply, and fill the earth still stood. (Genesis 1:28) The curse that fell upon them made life harder — like sailing a damaged vessel through rough seas — but it did not strip the pair of their Skipper-given dignity and purpose. They were pirates, aye, but Skipper kept an eye on 'em, and He promised always to love and bless 'em. Their full restoration lay ahead.

Free Will: The Gift That Comes with Weight

One of the most common questions people ask be this: if Skipper be loving, why does He allow suffering?

The answer begins with understanding one of the most significant gifts Skipper ever gave us — free will.

Skipper created every man and woman to be His image-bearers — sons of Skipper — capable of genuine love, real choice, and authentic relationship. But this freedom to love be also the freedom to reject love, reject Skipper, and continue sailing solo by our own wits. Skipper gave Adam and Eve the choice to trust Him or to go their own way — and He gives us the same choice today.

Think of it this way: Skipper handed us the helm and said, *"This vessel be yours. I've given ye everything ye need — the charts, the compass, and the open sea. But where ye sail be up to ye."* He does not override our choices, any more than a loving captain can grab the wheel every time a crewman steers recklessly. What we do — for good or ill — has consequences that ripple far beyond our own hull. Three sheets to the wind or sailing true, the choice be ours.

Skipper's sovereignty does not counter our free will. It cannot. His plans will come forth, but because He made us in His image with the ability to choose or reject, create or destroy, we determine our course, not Him. He calls. He counsels. He loves. But it be on us to receive.

But here be the good news: He does not abandon His purposes simply because we wander off course. He works through our choices — even our failures — to bring about His greater plan. Our failure and faulty plotting did not catch Skipper off guard. Redemption were already His intention.

Learning From Crew Who Came Before

The history of Skipper's people be, in many ways, a long and honest record of free will in action — with all its beauty and all its wreckage. Generation after generation, men and women with genuine faith made costly choices that left them — and others — dead in the water.

Abraham received one of the most extraordinary promises in Scripture: that through him and his wife, Sarah, Skipper would build a nation. But when years passed and Sarah remained childless, Abraham grew impatient. He took Hagar, Sarah's servant, as a concubine and fathered a son named Ishmael. The tension born from that decision has echoed through generations, right down to our own day. The animosity between those two brothers — Isaac and Ishmael, one free, one a slave — may one day lead to the end of all days. Abraham's impatience did not cancel Skipper's promise, but it created pain that could have been avoided. Leaving port before Skipper gives the order rarely ends cleanly. (Genesis 16)

Lot, a righteous man who traveled with Abraham and shared in his blessings, made a fateful decision when he chose to settle near Sodom, a city steeped in wickedness and morally bankrupt. Righteousness be not a shield against the slow corruption of a bad harbor. Lot lingered too long with the wrong crowd and remained in a corrupt port, and when Skipper's judgment finally fell on Sodom, Lot lost everything but his life and two daughters. A yellow-livered escape it were — he and his daughters barely made it out alive, and his wife didn't make it out at all on account of she looked back and became a condiment.

Where we choose to drop anchor matters enormously. (Genesis 13:12-13)

Jacob were a man of great destiny and deeply flawed character. He deceived his own father and cheated his brother Esau out of his birthright and blessing. His life were marked by strife and consequence — years of hard labor, family betrayal, and heartbreak. And yet Skipper remained faithful to Jacob, not because Jacob deserved it, but because Skipper's purposes be not dependent on our performance. Through Jacob's twelve sons came the twelve tribes of Israel — Skipper's covenant people. Flawed vessels. Faithful Skipper. (Genesis 27, 29:25)

Moses were chosen, favored, and uniquely positioned — raised in Pharaoh's own household, destined to deliver Israel from slavery. But Moses had a temper, and in a moment of anger, he killed an Egyptian and had to flee the country. That single act of unchecked rage — the act of a man gone three sheets to the wind with fury — delayed Israel's deliverance by decades. Even the most gifted and called among us can capsize others when we let our worst impulses take the helm. (Exodus 2:10-12)

The pattern be consistent and instructive, and no mistake: Skipper does not abandon His people when they fail. Our choices carry real weight, and they affect not only us but those sailing with us. Skipper be always looking for a way to right our wrongs. Trusting Skipper's timing — rather than forcing our own heading — be not passive. It be one of the most active and courageous things a new captain can do.

Redemption: A Full Refit

Through every failure, every act of rebellion, every consequence endured, one thread remained unbroken: Skipper's relentless pursuit of all rogue pirates who have gone astray.

The law given to Moses revealed the standard of holiness and our inability to meet it on our own. The prophets kept the flame of hope alive, pointing forward to the Son who were coming. And then — in the fullness of time — the Son arrived, and nothing were ever the same again.

The Son be the answer to every problem. Where Adam brought death through disobedience, the Son brought life through perfect obedience. Where sin had fractured our relationship with Skipper, the Son's death and resurrection tore down the barrier completely. He didn't come to patch a few leaks or slap on a fresh coat of paint. He came to make us entirely new — to restore us to the Shipwright's original design and then some, giving us life abundant — full, overflowing, and eternal. (John 10:10)

And before He ascended, He made a staggering declaration: *"All authority in heaven and on earth has been given to* ***me****. Therefore, ye go and make disciples of all nations."* (Matthew 28:18-19) He then promised that those who believe in Him would do even greater works than He had done, empowered by the same Holy Ghost of Truth that raised Him from the dead. (John 14:12)

This be the inheritance of every believer. This be what came with your new life when ye returned to Skipper and submitted to His counsel, love, and forgiveness.

Understanding Who Ye Be in the Son

Here be a picture worth sitting with.

Imagine a bottle floating in the ocean. The bottle be in the water. But some of the water also be *inside the bottle*. Now the bottle be not only in the water — the water be in the bottle. This be what it means to be in the Son, and to have the Son in ye.

Ye be the vessel. The Son be the ocean. And because His Holy Ghost of Truth dwells within ye, ye be not merely a passenger watching His work from the deck — ye be crew. Some believers carry only a splash of His presence, barely aware of the power available to them — sailing a mighty vessel and using it mainly to fish off the stern. Others be filled to the waterline, overflowing with His life, love, and authority.

The question worth asking be: how full be your hold?

Because the degree to which the Son fills your hold — to the degree He be the cargo ye carry — be the measure by which His power flows through ye. Believers have been given authority to heal, to break spiritual bondage, and to overcome the power of the enemy. Through the Holy Ghost of Truth, we also receive spiritual gifts — prophecy, miracles, and more — to be used as ambassadors of the Son, bringing His message of reconciliation, justice, and healing to the world. We carry the same commission, the same Holy Ghost of Truth, and through the Son, the same authority that Skipper originally granted to Adam, now fully restored. We carry not only the image of Skipper but His full nature.

Living the Abundant Life: Your Captain's Daily Orders

Authority without action be just potential. So what does it look like to actually sail this life well every day? Look alive, Mates — here be your orders.

Prayer. This be how ye stay connected to the source. Prayer be not a religious formality — it be a direct line to Skipper who built ye, loves ye, and has charted a course for your life. Think of prayer as a constant conversation on deck with the Shipwright — the Skipper of the fleet and the One to whom we'll one day give an accounting of how we transported and treated His goods: people. He knows every reef, every current, and every storm ahead. Through prayer, we access His wisdom, His strength, and His direction. When in doubt, shout out to Skipper.

Scripture. Skipper's Word be not a rulebook — it be your Captain's manual. It tells ye who Skipper be, who ye be in Him, and how this vessel were designed to sail. Feed on it consistently. Mark the passages that challenge ye, convict ye, and call ye to a better heading. A captain who never reads the manual will run aground, and often, ye may lay to that.

Community. Ye were never meant to sail alone. Believers need each other — to encourage, to pray, to sharpen, and to hold one another accountable. A ship needs a crew — every swabbie pulling his weight, every deck hand when the squall hits. Find your crew. Show up for 'em. Let 'em show up for ye.

Salt and Light. The Son called His followers to be salt and light in the world — preserving what be good, illuminating what be true, adding flavor and life to everything they touch. This be not passive sailing. It means standing up for justice in every port, caring for the poor when ye find 'em, tending to the sick, sharing the good news with strangers, and being the visible, tangible love of the Son to everyone in your wake. Ye be not sailing for yourself alone. Ye be sailing under the Cross of the Son — so be alert, stand your watch, and give a hand when ye can.

All Hands on Deck

The enemy dealt what looked like a fatal blow in the garden. But Skipper never abandoned his crew of two. No, sir.

Through the Son, everything that were lost has been reclaimed — and more. Ye carry the authority of the first Adam, restored and powered by the risen Son. Ye have been given gifts, weapons, and a Holy Ghost of Truth that the forces of darkness cannot overcome. By thunder, that be a commission worth sailing for.

So do not shrink back. Do not sit in port with your sails furled. Do not let the enemy convince ye that ye be just drifting, just surviving, just waiting for heaven.

Ye were made for abundant life — the kind that enjoys time, passages, and people, yes, but also enjoys sharing the blessings of Skipper. Be about His business.

Cast off and live the salt life!

The Quartermaster's Orders

Don't sail solo. The moment the promise of something more lures ye to cast off on your own, ye be headed for the same waters Adam and Eve found themselves in. Skipper gave ye the helm and everything ye need to sail well. Use it.

Watch where ye drop anchor. Lot were a righteous man who chose the wrong port and lingered too long — and it cost him nearly everything. Righteousness be not a shield against the slow rot of a bad harbor. Where ye put in matters. Choose with care.

Don't leave port before Skipper gives the order. Abraham's impatience created pain that could have been avoided and consequences that echo to this day. Skipper's timing be not our timing — but His timing be always right. Wait for the word.

Keep your worst impulses off the helm. One moment of unchecked rage cost Moses decades of delay for an entire nation. When fury, fear, or pride reach for the wheel, hold fast and let Skipper steady the course.

Ask yourself how full your hold be. The degree to which the Son fills your hold be the measure by which His power flows through ye. Don't settle for a splash. Get filled.

Keep the conversation going on deck. Prayer be a direct line to Skipper, who built ye, knows every reef ahead, and has charted your course. Keep the line open.

Feed on His Word. It tells ye who ye be in the Son and how this vessel were designed to sail. A captain who never reads the manual will run aground. Let it work on ye through the day.

Find your crew and show up for 'em. Ye were never meant to make this passage alone. Find your people. Show up for 'em. Let 'em show up for ye.

Be salt and light in every port. Stand up for justice. Care for the poor. Tend to the sick. Be the visible love of the Son to everyone in your wake.

Don't sit in port with your sails furled. Through the Son, everything lost has been reclaimed — and more. Ye carry the authority of the first Adam, restored and powered by the risen Son. Gifts, weapons, and a Holy Ghost of Truth that the forces of darkness cannot overcome. That be a commission worth sailing for.

Pirate Facts

Folks from all walks of life came to be pirates — not just your murdering, lying, thieving scoundrels and bilge rats. The pirate William Kidd were a young lad from a wealthy family who later took up pirating whilst on a mission to hunt pirates, and were executed for the very crime he set out to stop. Whilst ye be seeking to root out sin in others, take care ye don't get entangled in it yourself.

Chapter Two

Skipper's Law of Love

Port Royal, Jamaica. 1673. Or thereabouts: The sun be hammering the docks with the full force of a ship's surgeon pounding a peg leg in place on a man who be not entirely certain the peg be the correct length. Somewhere amidst the sweltering heat of that wicked, glorious port — the most sinful city in the New World, they called it — a Dutchman named Rock Braziliano be drinking himself senseless.

Again.

> *"If one thing more be necessary, then when the Son says, 'It is finished,' He be lying — for one thing more means a thing not be complete."*

Ye know his type. They be in every port. Big. Loud. Rank as bilge water. Often singing off-key a James Delaney tune while feasting on a free buffet.

The pirate Rock of Brazil had once roasted two farmers alive on wooden spits simply because they wouldn't hand over their pigs — a negotiating style that, while effective in the short term, did little for his reputation as a dinner guest. He'd terrorize crews into drinking with him at knifepoint. He proved himself to be a drunken, debauched, cruel scoundrel beyond the measure that even hardened buccaneers found comfortable. He were not the kind of man ye invited to supper — unless ye wished to be the main dish. Aye, he were the kind of man who showed up unannounced, ate every morsel, drank the grog locker dry, and then threatened to shoot the cook and quartermaster unless he got his fill.

By any reasonable measure, Rock of Brazil were done for. Not just legally — though the Spanish had already clapped him in irons once — but morally. Spiritually. A man were so far from the shores of decency that no self-respecting preacher would welcome him into their home, their church, or a Sunday homecoming — particularly not one near a spit.

And yet.

Skipper looked at Rock of Brazil and said: *This one, I'll snatch from the flames of the fire pit he stocks and save.*

A Roasting Spit of a Different Sort

Picture the motley crew gathered in Antioch. Young, naive, still finding her sea legs. Jewish believers and Gentile believers alike. Congregants from wildly divergent backgrounds and traditions, and sailing under different colours. And yet, somehow, they found themselves eating at the same tables, worshipping the same risen Christ. It be a small miracle to which every soul could attest.

Simon were there. The Rock, the one the Son once declared, would become the foundation for the church. A man of convictions. A chap whose words often led to a rebuke and then some. A fellow who kept a tight rein on things. Always had. Always would. And for a while, he were doing a fine job keeping tempers tamped down at this feast.

He were eating with the Gentile believers freely, openly, and without hesitation. Having received a vision from Skipper telling him that nothing be unclean — that Skipper has declared clean — The Rock knows this. Mark it well: he *knows* this. And yet...

When a group of Jewish Christians arrives from Jerusalem — men closely associated with James, pillars of the church, and Jews to boot — Peter takes leave of the Gentiles. He excuses himself and moves to a different table. He didn't make a scene of it; he just eased into picking sides slowly, returning to old habits, preferring one group over the next. Judging one class better than another. One race, one skin color as his own preferred — as though Skipper had said as much — when He did not.

The rest of the Jewish believers follow his lead. Even Barnabas were swept away by this current that smacks of the *Haves* and *Half-knots.*

Paul clapped eyes on the hypocrisy — the aloof posture of the pious Jews sent by James, Jesus' brother — and he called the crew to task.

He confronted Peter to his face. Right there before the whole crew. Not because Peter simply were two-faced and wrong, but because what Peter were doing in that moment were planting the seeds of death in their midst. This cancer — *kosher food only, obedience to the old ways always* — if left to take root, will destroy the Brethren. By separating himself, Peter were sending the message that to be fully accepted, ye need Jesus Christ the Son plus one thing more. One more act of purity. One more ritual of righteousness.

And that, Paul made clear, scuttles Jesus' sacrifice on the cross. If one thing more be necessary, then when the

Son says, "It is finished," He be lying, for one thing more means a thing not be complete.

Paul says plain: "I do not set aside the grace of Skipper. Nay, if righteousness could be gained through the law, then Christ died for nothing" (Galatians 2:21).

That confrontation in Antioch be the heartbeat behind Paul's entire letter to the Galatians, where he writes: "Clearly no one who relies on the law is justified before Skipper, because the righteous will live by faith." (Galatians 3:11)

Which be to say: Skipper gave His people laws and commands, but no one were able to keep all of them. Some do better than others, by a long sea-mile, but all fall short. And not by a little.

To those insisting that salvation required Christ — *plus* keeping the law — Paul delivers this verdict: "You have been ***alienated*** from Christ. You have ***fallen away from grace***." (Galatians 5:4)

Let that sink in, mates. Set apart: not for good works or the glory of Skipper, but because such works are dead. Dry. Withered. And destined for the fire pit.

Not because The Code be bad. The Code be good. The Code stands (Romans 7:16). But Jesus fulfilled all the law, in order that we might live by grace, not as slaves under the law. The moment ye add anything to Christ as a condition of salvation, ye have said He be not enough. And if He be not enough, then the cross be but an empty mainmast.

No Jesus. No sails to be filled. No way to reach your home port of Paradise.

What Do We Do With the Law?

So do we throw The Code overboard? *Blast ye, by no means!*

Jesus answers plain: "Until heaven and earth disappear, not the smallest letter, not the least stroke of a pen, will by any means disappear from the Law until everything is accomplished." (Matthew 5:18) The earth remains. The Code remains: not to save us from sin, for The Code cannot save. In fact, the power of sin be in the law, and sin leads to death. (1 Corinthians 15:56)

This Code, Chart, and Compass. All three be necessary for skillful navigation.

The Code be Skipper's written word: Jesus in words. All the nature and character of Skipper and the Son be reflected in The Code. The Chart derives its longitudes and latitudes from The Code. You set a heading based on coordinates that align with Lat and Long. Can't find the Lat and Long for your heading? Then it's not a place on the chart where you can sail. Least ways, not from Skipper's purview of matters. The Code, Chart, and your inner Compass, Skipper's Holy Spirit, keep you on course.

But mark it well: a compass heading cannot account for what the sea does to ye be underway. There 'ill be times when ye need to fall off to account for headers:

to sail away from stiff currents, slowing your progress. Your heading be fixed, but it be you on the helm, so make course adjustments as need be, but always return to a heading that'll take you to your destination. Wind, waves, currents... these be the sufferings and persecutions Paul speaks of. But such do not stop a sailor with a fixed eye on his port.

And here be where the metaphor bites hardest. Peter in Antioch were that sailor. The Rock knew The Code: purity. Nothing unclean. He knew the Lat and Long required no "dogs." No Gentiles. But his Compass spun him wildly away from the course he set. And that were where Paul stepped in to show how The Rock was fighting the wind — Skipper's Holy Spirit — and that was a way to reach holiness that did not involve rejecting men and women of different colours, countries, and character.

The Spirit of Christ sets the same destination for all: holiness. But no amount of tacking, steering, or sheeting in sails will take us there on our own account. Aye, we must lay aside our efforts and let Jesus be our holiness. Let Him be our righteousness. When we surrender the helm to Him, He makes us holy, righteous, and keeps us in good standing with Skipper.

This be the new law: The Code of the Spirit of life (Romans 8:2), The Code of Christ (Galatians 6:2), Paul speaks of. We stop trying in our own effort and let His Holy Spirit fill our sails with His purity and perfection.

When Skipper looks at ye, He sees His Son Jesus, not your shabby self. Think on that a wee bit. Ye be so swallowed up in Christ, the Father ONLY sees His Son Jesus. Our small selves be but a speck amidst the glory of Christ, and yet we specks be made perfect, holy, and righteous 'cause we be in Him.

In Christ, through His Spirit, we keep the old law: not by grinding out obedience against the weather, but because Christ kept all the law. He did not sin, so we do not sin. His Spirit lives in us (Romans 8:3–4), so our spirit lives in Him. This obedience earns us no extra grace, love, mercy, or merit, but instead produces in us fruit that blesses others: love, joy, peace, patience, kindness, generosity, and loyalty to Skipper. (Galatians 5:22–23)

If ye accept Christ, will ye still sin? Aye, if ye believe ye will — if ye want to enjoy the pleasures of sin. No, if ye accept that ye be not obligated to sin.

Can ye go the rest of yer life without sinning? Try. Right now. Begin this very moment. Declare: *I will not sin.* Count to five. Did ye sin in the last five seconds? No? Count to ten. Did ye make it? Count to one hundred. Still sinless? Now think on this: Had ye died before reaching one hundred, ye would have lived without sinning again. Perhaps this seems like foolish talk, but living holy be living one moment at a time.

This be the holy life: a life fixed not on sin, but on Jesus. A life that allows His Spirit to live fully in us.

Guilt comes from the law, and we be free from the law. Regret be fine. Wanting to do better, be right. But never allow guilt to persuade ye that ye be unworthy in Skipper's eyes. Never assume that when ye sin, Skipper loves ye less. He loves ye the same when ye sin and when ye don't — because when He looks at ye, He sees Christ. And that be ***all*** He sees. (2 Corinthians 5:21)

Ye Be Crew

Once ye accept Christ, ye be signed on as crew aboard Skipper's vessel. Nothing ye do can get ye thrown off the ship. It doesn't matter if ye be still learning the rigging, keep coiling the ropes the wrong way, or accidentally let the anchor line run out too fast and far. He does not cast ye onto a remote island and leave ye marooned from His crew. Ye sail under the flag of Jesus — not skull and crossbones — and that tells Skipper everything He needs to know.

Ye belong to Him. Ye be on His ship. (Romans 8:38–39)

And because Skipper be patient and generous — and because His Holy Spirit be in your heart — ye ***will*** become a better sailor. We be not free to sin; we be free to sail in Him. (Galatians 5:13) Feed on the ship's bread each day — Jesus — and ye will avoid sin. And when ye feed on Him daily, The Code becomes a pleasure to hold true.

Jesus knew The Code, lived The Code, and yet was not constrained by The Code. He understood the holiness of the Sabbath and kept it — not through rigid obedience to steps and lifting and plucking heads of grain — but in the love, mercy, grace, and obedience that comes from loving Skipper and your neighbor as yourself. (Matthew 22:39)

Paul states it plain: *"Live by the Spirit"* (Galatians 5:16) and sail in victory.

If ye sail by the Spirit's leading, ye will sail true. Ye may lay to that.

The End of Rock of Brazil

If Rock Braziliano had been the only soul on earth who would ever accept the grace and mercy of Skipper through Jesus Christ, the only one, the sole taker, but a single sorry wretch in all of creation who said, "Yes! Save me!" — the Father would still have sent His Son. To suffer. To bleed. To die. He'd do it again without flinching. That's how much he loves each of us — loves you.

Rock Braziliano disappeared from the historical record around 1673. We don't know how he died. We don't know what he thought about in the dark hours when the rum wore off and the night came on long and quiet. We don't know if, in some forgotten moment in some forgotten corner of that wicked, glorious port, he ever looked up.

But the door stood open. All the way to the end. It was open the day he roasted those farmers. It was open the day the Spanish threw him in irons. It was open every single rum-soaked, blood-stained morning of his life. Maybe Rock Braziliano called Jesus before he died.

Jesus stands at the door and knocks. But He's not rude. He only comes in by invitation.

Invite Him in this day.

Pirate Facts

The Quartermaster be a high calling aboard any vessel. During times of battle, the Captain holds unlimited authority, but at other times he and the rest of the crew be subject ter the command of the Quartermaster. It be his (or her) duty ter represent the crew's interests. For this, the Quartermaster receives an extra share of the booty when it be divided. *More treasure!* Above all, the Quartermaster protects the crew from each other by maintaining order, settling quarrels, and distributing food and other essentials. A jury of the crew tries serious crimes, but the Quartermaster has the authority ter punish each feller fer minor offenses. If the crew be successful in their attack on a vessel, the Quartermaster decides what plunder to take from a prize. If the pirates decided to keep a captured ship, the Quartermaster will assume command till the vessel be disposed of. The crew elects the Quartermaster immediately after choosing a Captain.

Chapter Three

Genuine Faith and Explosive Power

The Captain Who Flew the Wrong Colors

There be an old and terrible practice in the history of piracy called sailing under false colors.

> *"Ye cannot fake a wake. The water doesn't lie."*

A pirate vessel would approach a merchant ship flying the flag of a friendly nation — Britain, Spain, Portugal, whoever the merchant captain trusted. The merchant would see the colors, relax his guard, and allow the ship to come alongside. And at the last possible moment, just as the hulls were nearly touching, the false flag would come down, and the black flag would go up.

The merchant captain, at this point, would experience a sudden and dramatic reassessment of his career path.

The sailors who practiced this were not simply thieves. They were something more unsettling — they were counterfeits. They had mastered the appearance of something they were not. They could sail the ship, speak the language, and wear the uniform. From a distance — even from a fairly close distance — ye could not tell the difference.

Jesus describes something eerily similar in the most sobering passage in the entire Gospels.

> *"Not everyone who says to me, 'Lord, Lord,' will enter the kingdom of heaven, but only the one who does the will of my Father who is in heaven. Many will say to me on that day, 'Lord, Lord, did we not prophesy in your name and in your name drive out demons and in your name perform many miracles?' Then I will tell them plainly, 'I never knew you. Away from me, you evildoers!'"* (Matthew 7:21-23)

Read that again slowly.

These be not people who rejected Jesus. These be people who served in His name. They prophesied. They drove out demons. They performed miracles. From every external angle, they looked like the real thing. They had the right flag flying. They spoke the right language. They were doing the work.

And Jesus says: I never knew you.

Not, "I knew ye once, but ye drifted away." Not, "I knew ye, but ye sinned too much."

Never.

This be the most important question any person on this voyage can answer: Does Jesus know me? Not "Do I know about Jesus?" Not "Have I done things in Jesus' name?" But does He know me? Be there something real between us, something alive, something that goes deeper than the flag I fly?

This section be about that question. And the answer, by Skipper's grace, be available to everyone.

Ye Must Be Born Again

Imagine a sailor who has spent his entire life studying the sea.

He has read every chart, memorized every tide table, and passed every examination. He can tell ye the depth of any major harbor, the pattern of trade winds in every season, and the history of every significant naval battle ever fought. He knows the sea in every way that can be known from dry land, which is to say he knows almost nothing about the sea.

And has never once been on a ship.

He has never felt the deck move beneath his feet. Never smelled salt air at four in the morning. Never had the wheel in his hands in a following sea. Never known what it be to be genuinely, completely, terrifyingly at the mercy of something larger than himself — and discover in that moment that he be held.

All his knowledge be real. None of his experience be.

This be the difference between knowing about Jesus and being born of His Spirit.

Nicodemus were a Pharisee — one of the most educated, most devout, most religiously accomplished men in Israel. He came to Jesus at night, perhaps to avoid being seen, and opened the conversation with a compliment: *"Rabbi, we know that you are a teacher who has come from God."* He were acknowledging Jesus' credentials. He were speaking the language of scholarship and theology.

Jesus cuts straight through it.

> *"Very truly I tell you, no one can see the kingdom of God unless they are born again."* (John 3:3)

Nicodemus were baffled. *"How can someone be born when they are old?"*

He were thinking about the natural world — the only world his scholarship had prepared him for. Jesus be talking about something that no amount of study can produce:

> *"Flesh gives birth to flesh, but the Spirit gives birth to spirit."* (John 3:6)

Ye cannot think your way into the kingdom. Ye cannot study your way in. Ye cannot perform your way in, or serve your way in, or impress your way in. Ye must be born of water and Spirit: by the washing of rebirth and renewal that only the Holy Spirit can accomplish. (Titus 3:5)

This be not a theological technicality. It be the difference between a man who has memorized every chart and a man who has actually been to sea. One has information. The other has been changed.

The New Creation — Old Cargo Thrown Overboard

When a vessel be taken as a prize and brought under new ownership, the first thing the new captain does be inspect the hold.

Whatever cargo the old owner were carrying — whether contraband, rot, or simply goods that have no place in the new vessel's mission — it gets thrown overboard. The ship be the same. The hull, the masts, and the rigging be unchanged. But what the vessel carries, and where it be going, be entirely different now.

This be what the new birth does to a human soul.

> *"If anyone is in Christ, the new creation has come: The old has gone, the new is here!"* (2 Corinthians 5:17)

The old cargo — the shame, the patterns, the allegiances, the appetites that were slowly sinking the vessel — begins to go. Not all at once, perhaps. The hold be deep, and some of it were stored a long time ago. But the new Captain has taken the helm, and He be thorough. Patient. Relentless in the best possible way.

> *"If anyone does not have the Spirit of Christ, he does not belong to Christ."* (Romans 8:9)

This be the diagnostic. Not, "Do ye attend church?" Not, "Do ye use the right vocabulary?" Not, "Do ye perform the right religious functions?" Does the Spirit of Christ live in ye? Be He moving in your hold, rearranging things, throwing out what doesn't belong, making room for what does?

The characteristics of a vessel under new management be not subtle over time. Forgiveness replaces bitterness. Compassion replaces contempt. Humility replaces the need to be right. Peace — real peace, not the absence of trouble but the presence of Skipper in the middle of trouble — begins to steady the hull in weather that would have capsized the old life.

This be not self-improvement. A man cannot renovate his own hull from the inside while he be sailing. This be the work of the Spirit — the divine Shipwright, coming aboard, doing what only He can do.

The Wind and the Captain — Living a Spirit-Led Life

A sailing vessel without wind be a beautiful, useless thing.

She can have the finest hull ever laid, the best rigging money can buy, and a captain of extraordinary skill and experience. And she will go nowhere. She will sit in the harbor, impressive and motionless, until either the wind comes or she rots at the dock.

The Holy Spirit be the wind. And a Spirit-led life be what happens when a vessel stops trying to row itself across the ocean and learns instead to raise its sails.

> *"Those who are led by the Spirit of God are the children of God."* (Romans 8:14)

A Spirit-led life be not passive — raising a sail requires knowledge, skill, and constant attention. Ye have to know how to trim it for the conditions. Ye have to be willing to adjust when the wind shifts. Ye have to trust, when the wind takes ye in a direction ye didn't plan, that the One who sends the wind knows the destination better than ye do.

But the power be not yours. It never were. The moment ye stop straining at the oars and open yourself to the wind, something changes. The vessel moves in ways that have nothing to do with your own strength. People around ye begin to feel the draft of something they cannot fully explain. They be feeling the wind of the Spirit moving through a life that has learned to sail by it.

This be what it looks like in practice: loving people who be difficult to love, because the Spirit loves through ye. Forgiving offenses that your natural self would hold forever, because the Spirit has given ye a new capacity. Serving without applause, giving without calculation, speaking truth without cruelty — because the One who does all these things perfectly has taken up residence in your heart and be slowly, gloriously remaking ye in His image.

> *"The fruit of the Spirit is love, joy, peace, forbearance, kindness, goodness, faithfulness, gentleness, and self-control."* (Galatians 5:22-23)

Ye cannot manufacture this fruit. Ye can fake it for a season, the way a ship can fly false colors for a while. But genuine fruit, borne of the genuine Spirit, be something different entirely. It grows. It deepens. It shows up in the dark as well as in the light, in the storm as well as in the calm. And unlike the performance of the religious counterfeit, it does not require an audience.

Known by Name — The Heart of Genuine Faith

Now we come to the deepest thing.

All the fruit, all the transformation, all the Spirit-led sailing — none of it be the point in itself. It be all the evidence of something beneath it, something more fundamental than behavior or gift or performance.

It be a relationship.

Jesus, on the night before His crucifixion, prays for His disciples — and for every person who would ever believe through their message — with words that should make every follower of Christ stop breathing for a moment:

> *"Father, just as you are in me and I am in you, may they also be in us."* (John 17:21)

Read that again. He be not praying that we would follow Him from a respectful distance. He be not praying that we would perform well in His service or represent His cause faithfully. He be praying that we would be in them — in the Father and the Son — the way the Father be in the Son and the Son be in the Father.

This be not the language of an employer and an employee. It be not the language of a king and a subject. It be the language of family. Of union. Of the kind of knowing that goes bone deep, that cannot be faked, that be not built on what ye have done but on who ye be to each other.

This be what Jesus means when He says, *"I never knew you"* to the workers of miracles. He be not saying He never observed them. He be saying there were never this — never the intimate union of a soul abiding in Him and Him abiding in that soul. They were working for Him without ever being with Him.

> *"Whoever believes in me will do the works I have been doing, and they will do even greater things than these."* (John 14:12)

The works flow from the relationship. Not the other way around. Ye do not perform your way into intimacy with Jesus. Ye abide in Him, and the works come as naturally as fruit comes from a branch that be drawing life from the vine.

How do ye cultivate this intimacy? The same way any relationship deepens: time, attention, honesty, trust. Prayer — not the recitation of words, but genuine conversation with the One who already knows everything about ye and loves ye anyway. Solitude — the quiet place where the noise of the world fades, and ye can actually hear. The Word — not as a textbook but as a love letter, as a conversation, as the living voice of the One who made ye and be making ye still.

> *"You have been born again… through the living and enduring word of God."* (1 Peter 1:23)

> *"The Word became flesh and made his dwelling among us."* (John 1:14)

The written Word and the living Word be inseparable. When ye open the Bible and ask the Holy Spirit to speak, Jesus Himself be in the room. Ye be not studying a historical document. Ye be sitting with the Author. And the Author be not finished with ye yet.

By Their Fruit Ye Will Know Them

In the end, the question be not what flag ye fly. It be not what words ye speak, what title ye carry, or what works ye have performed.

It be what grows in your wake.

"By their fruit you will recognize them." (Matthew 7:20)

A vessel under genuine wind produces a genuine wake. The sea behind a Spirit-filled life tells the story — transformed relationships, healed wounds, restored hope, lives touched and changed by an overflow of what the Spirit has poured in. Ye cannot fake a wake. The water doesn't lie.

And the fruit goes deeper than what others can see. It shows up in how ye treat the person who cannot help ye. In how ye respond when no one be watching. In what ye do with failure — whether it drives ye to shame and hiding, or back to the One whose grace be new every morning.

> *"Children born not of natural descent... but born of God."* (John 1:13)

This be who ye be — if the Spirit of Christ lives in ye. Not a sailor trying to earn his berth. Not a deckhand performing tricks to impress the Captain. A child of Skipper, born of His Spirit, sailing in His name, toward a destination that He has been preparing since before the world were made.

Do Not Settle for False Colors

The most sobering truth in all of this be also the most merciful.

Jesus did not say, *"I never knew you,"* to people who had already received His Spirit and been born again. He said it to people who had the form of faith without the substance — who had done the work without ever entering the relationship. The warning be not for those who be in Him. It be a lighthouse for those who be still sailing toward the wrong harbor under the wrong flag, thinking they be safe when they be not.

If ye be reading this and something in your spirit be unsettled — good. That unsettled feeling may be the Holy Spirit doing what He does: convicting, drawing, calling ye to something more than religious performance.

Do not settle for flying false colors. Do not trade the real thing for a convincing imitation.

Seek the Spirit. Ask to be filled. Open the hold to the new Captain. Let the old cargo go. Raise your sails to the wind of the Spirit and let Him take ye where no amount of rowing could ever reach.

Be known by Jesus.

That be the whole voyage. That be the treasure.

Everything else be just sailing.

Pirate Facts

The ship's Carpenter — also known as the surgeon — be responsible for the maintenance and repair of the hull, masts, and yards. He or she works under the direction of the ship's Master and Boatswain. The Carpenter's duties be to check the hull regularly, placing oakum between the seams of the planks and wooden plugs on leaks to keep the vessel tight. The Carpenter may also serve as the ship's Surgeon and perform amputations (and other operations) with the same woodworking tools he or she uses to repair the ship — a fact that patients were generally not informed of in advance.

Chapter Four

Baptism Into Christ: Getting Under Way

Bartholomew Sharp never expected to get a second chance.

> *"Every charge. Gone. His record wiped clean — a new commission in hand. That be the power of a pardon, Mates."*

He had risen to command almost by accident — sailing with a crew of buccaneers off the coast of South America when they needed a captain. Sharp stepped up and proved himself smart as paint

— which, among buccaneers, be a notably low bar. He cleared with room to spare and became a natural leader and a skilled seaman, and for a time, the prizes came in abundance.

Then, in January 1681, his crew turned on him. A mutiny stripped him of his command and tossed him overboard. Most men would have swum for shore, taken up a quieter profession, and never once looked back. But Sharp was no lily-livered swab. Three weeks later, when his replacement was killed, the crew came back to where he sat resting under the shade of a palm tree. He took the helm again without a word of complaint and kept sailing.

Under his second command, the buccaneers seized twenty-five Spanish ships and plundered settlements up and down the South American coast. But when the voyage was done, and Sharp made port back in England, he faced a piracy charge that might soon see him dancing the hempen jig.

Sharp, though, had something tucked in his frock that changed his fortunes. During the voyage, he had seized a priceless book of Spanish navigational charts — *Waggoner of the South Seas* — detailing waters no English sailor had ever mapped. He laid it before King Charles II, who, upon clapping eyes on navigational charts of waters no Englishman had ever mapped, immediately discovered that piracy be a significantly more complicated moral question than he had previously considered. The king granted Sharp a full royal pardon.

Every charge. Gone. His record wiped clean—a new commission in hand.

That be the power of a pardon, Mates. And that be precisely what Jesus, the Son of God, offers. In Him, we be fully pardoned from all offenses — those we did in the past, those we will do in the future. In Christ, we live in eternity's time, so past, present, and future be one.

But the pardon is only the beginning. Before ye can set sail for Paradise — that home you've always sought but couldn't plot on a chart — ye must be born of the Holy Ghost of Truth. This be how ye take possession of all the riches of Christ Jesus. All that's offered through that sure anchor — hope for today, provision for tomorrow, and life forever — starts here, with new life in Him.

The Holy Ghost of Truth came upon Mary, and through Him, Jesus was conceived. This be how we get born again. His Holy Ghost of Truth comes upon us, conceives Christ within us, and transforms our old spirit into His. We be born into Skipper's family. His Holy Ghost of Truth connects with ours and provides an eternal link, bringing heaven to earth in us (1 Corinthians 6:17). Only then can we launch into a new life bound for Paradise.

What follows is our boarding, provisioning, and departing as a new, re-christened vessel. Each act is distinct. Together, they tell a single love story — one where the Son and Skipper demonstrate their love for us and how deeply they desire to bring us back to our true home port.

Be ye sure ye've received His Holy Ghost of Truth? Born by His Holy Ghost of Truth? If not, find a quiet place on deck or below, drop to your knees, and pray. Believe in your heart that the Son is Lord of all — be *your* Lord. Believe it. Go deep and expose your heart. Ask Skipper to speak His living word over you. Let His love confirm in your spirit that His Son died for your sins to save you. Be convinced of this. Know that the Son rose from the grave.

The evidence, by a long sea-mile, points in one direction — that Jesus rose from the dead.

Think of Mary, the mother of Jesus. She could have stopped His execution with these words: *"Joseph is his father!"* If this were true — if Mary and Joseph conceived Jesus — then Skipper was not His father. Mary would have conceived out of wedlock and lived a lie. But ask yourself: what mother would allow her son to be tortured and die an excruciating death simply to conceal her secret? Though bearing a child out-of-wedlock may carry its shame, only a reprobate mother would allow her firstborn to die in such a gruesome manner rather than speak one sentence of truth.

Think of His disciples. If the Son did not rise from the dead, they went to their deaths — tortured, beheaded, run through with the sword, doused in flames — for a lie. What was their gain? Fame? Position? Power? No. Persecution. What man would die for a lie that cost him everything and gained him nothing? A lie that placed his family at risk of death and persecution?

Think of James, the brother of the Son. James didn't believe his brother was the Messiah until after His death. What changed his mind? Stories? Miracles? All such were in the past. Only an encounter with the risen Son — his own half-brother — could have persuaded James to abandon his entrenched beliefs and accept that his older brother was conceived by the Holy Ghost of Truth.

Get this settled first — and ye may lay to it — the Son was the Son of Skipper. He died. He rose three days later. He fulfilled every prophecy about the Messiah. Once this belief becomes your conviction, confess it to someone — even aloud to yourself — that the Son is Lord of your life. That be saving grace.

Once done, produce fruit in keeping with true repentance and faith (Matthew 3:8). Repentance is sincere regret: a genuine turning away from what was toward what will be.

Now that you've shifted the course of your life, one of your first acts is to acknowledge the old habits, desires, and ways that need to change. Make a list — not so that ye will work to change, but so ye can track the changes the Son's Holy Ghost of Truth will make in you. Safe sailing begins with sound seamanship, and the Son now stands the helm. Mark it well. Every mate who doesn't produce good fruit will see his works tossed into the fire — and himself likewise, if he's not in the Son (Matthew 3:10).

Cut down the mainmast if it be rotten. Mizzenmast, too, if need be. The foremast is not exempt from this process, and neither, frankly, be the cook with the peg leg if he be serving up turtle entrails, again.

Think of the Holy Ghost of Truth as a firm but fair sailing master. When the Son speaks of fruit, He be talking about the grub ye dispense to the crew in your daily voyage — from the moment ye rise to the moment ye rest, serve the best. Picture yourself sailing into a new life. What kind of entries do ye wish to see written in the logbook each day? That ye dispensed patience, kindness, mercy? Compassion, encouragement, comfort, and the power of Skipper in your life? Make that list. Then track your results.

Baptism by Water

Your new birth is only the beginning of boarding. Ye have your list of old ways and habits. Ye have your list of bad fruit to toss out and good fruit to produce. But is your vessel — your soul — seaworthy?

Consider that the Son's first miracle was performed at a wedding — a public, joyous, festive occasion. So too is water baptism.

Baptism by water is your wedding ceremony — the moment ye stand before witnesses and declare what has already happened in your heart. Ye be a new creation in love with your Creator. It be a celebration. And like any wedding, it calls for wine. But not old wine. New wine. Holy Ghost of Truth wine.

Water baptism is not a mystical mystery — it is a visible mark on your hull, your soul, that declares: *this vessel has been claimed, commissioned, and launched into the fleet of Skipper.* Its importance is so great that the Son — even though He had no sin to repent of — was baptized, for it was proper for Him to do so to fulfill all righteousness (Matthew 3:15).

If ye haven't been baptized by water, make it a priority. Find a pastor and some folks and get that hull marked. Public or private, once done, ye will never forget the day.

In Cana, during that first miracle, the wine ran out. The initial joy of the wedding could not be sustained on its own; more was needed. And the Son provided. He filled empty vessels to the brim and beyond, turning plain water into the finest wine. He didn't offer just enough. He offered the best. This be what awaits those who wish to enjoy the fullness of the Son — not a half-filled life, but one running over.

Baptism by the Holy Ghost of Truth

John the Baptist said, *"Jesus will baptize you with fire and the Holy Spirit"* (Matthew 3:11). The wedding is done. Now comes the honeymoon. This be where we get wind in our sails, and the passage goes from sitting in the doldrums to flying across open seas. The Holy Ghost of Truth is explosive power, fire, and the level of living Jesus promised all who would ask.

The Son fills empty vessels to overflowing. This be the baptism of the Holy Ghost of Truth: being filled to the point where, as on the day of Pentecost, those who witnessed it thought the disciples were drunk — three sheets to the wind. That be a picture of someone so filled with His Holy Ghost of Truth that they be bold, loud, and perhaps overwhelming — someone so overcome by the Holy Ghost of Truth that others can't help but take notice.

In this baptism, the Groom comes fully into the one He loves.

He pours Himself into each one who asks. We be the bride, the one who receives. He be our Groom, the one who gives. And as our Groom, He keeps nothing back, nothing in reserve. He gave His all and gives His all, that we might live with the full abundance of life that comes with the riches of His glory.

In your old life, ye were adrift. And if honest, deep down, ye may have wondered if your life mattered. In this new life — filled each day with His Holy Ghost of Truth — every day matters. Every person matters. Because ye know in your soul that ye matter, and that ye were made for something larger and grander than anything ye can imagine.

Solitude no longer leads to loneliness, but to peace and confidence. Over time, you'll find that ye don't need to be noticed. Your satisfaction will come from knowing that the burden of holding course, trimming sails, and battling the elements no longer rests on ye alone. It rests on the Son, the One at the helm. And He be mighty pleased with you. Why? Because now ye be not simply made in the image of God; ye be being remade into the image of Christ.

Ask the Son to fill ye with His Holy Ghost of Truth. Wait. Listen. You'll know He's arrived when ye sense His presence and power rising within ye like wind filling a sail. Often warmth comes, a rising wholeness that leads to tears. When His Holy Ghost of Truth comes upon you, open your mouth and utter sounds, any sounds, and expect His language to change your natural noise into His holy language. This be your honeymoon night with your Groom. And oh, what an awesome moment it be. Write the date down — because if ye be like many, ye may not recall the exact date, but ye will always remember the moment the Son's Holy Ghost of Truth filled ye to the full.

Let Him Take the Helm

Now the Son's Holy Ghost of Truth is guiding ye (Matthew 4:1). Many will be the days when He steers ye into unfamiliar waters and desolate-feeling straits. Ye might think you've gone off course. But as long as the Son is with you, ye be never lost at sea. Though ye once stood the helm, now He charts your course. Some days, the most faithful thing ye can do is walk the deck, admire the view, and relish the knowledge that He navigates your life.

Water. Wind. Sails. Hoist your sails. Submit your will to His. Allow His breath to fill ye and send ye toward new horizons.

The Quartermaster's Orders

Do ye feel pardoned, forgiven, or still hold guilt and shame?

Write down your answer: "Do I believe Jesus rose from the dead?" Don't rush it. Sit with the evidence. Let it become conviction, not just agreement. Next **List:**

Old habits, desires, and ways ye know need to change. The fruit ye want your daily logbook to show.

If ye haven't been baptized by water, write down the name of one person ye can contact this week to make it happen. Set a date. Make it a celebration.

Find a quiet place. Ask the Son to fill ye with His Holy Ghost of Truth. Wait. Listen. Write down what happens, even if it feels small or uncertain. Date it.

PIRATE FACTS

"Avast ye!" be Dutch for "pay attention, Mates!" That be your charge today. Pay attention to what Skipper is saying to ye through His words and this message.

Chapter Five

The Difference Between "Born Again," and "Filled With the Holy Spirit"

Most men who turned to pirating did so out of desperation.

Poverty, oppression, abduction by marauding gangs on the docks: the grinding cruelty of the life of a lubber. All such drove men to the sea in search of something better — a share of the prize, a voice among the crew, a life of prestige, power, aye, even fame. For these men, piracy were not a passing fancy, but a conviction. They had the heart of a murdering, thieving scoundrel before they ever clapped eyes on a black flag.

> *"The difference between the wind of the Holy Ghost of Truth and saved-but-working-in-our-own-strength be the difference between a ship sailing and a crew rowing."*

But Stede Bonnet came to pirating from a different tack.

Born into wealth on the island of Barbados, Bonnet were a plantation owner and magistrate — respected, comfortable, and by every outward measure, a man who had already had what many a poor pirate sought. But something restless stirred in him, and in 1717 he did what no pirate before or since had done. He bought his own ship — rather than steal one — as any self-respecting pirate would have done. He named her the *Revenge* — which, given that his wife had announced under no uncertain terms that he would not be buying a boat, were either a statement of defiance or a confession of domestic reality, depending on which end of the marriage ye were standing. He hired a crew, outfitted her, and sailed off to steal, pillage, and plunder. Not because he needed to. Not because he were desperate, but because he fancied the idea of it.

He had the vessel. He had the colors. What he lacked were the heart of a pirate.

His crew barely respected him. He lacked the basic skills and seamanship of a chap who'd spent years at sea. So, when he fell in with Blackbeard, thinking he'd found a kindred spirit, Edward Teache simply took over the *Revenge*, crew and all — which, among pirates, be considered a perfectly reasonable response to meeting someone new.

Eventually, he became a captive to the spirit of piracy he so desperately wished to have.

In 1718 he were captured, escaped, and recaptured, and finally hanged in Charleston. He had everything a pirate needed — except the heart of a pirate.

A man who plays at faith in Jesus the way Bonnet played at piracy may one day find that he too has lost it all: his faith, his flock, and his crew.

This business of sailing with Skipper be not for the faint of heart, ye may lay to that. Jesus makes it clear: the world will hate ye. The beam of a cross will be laid across your shoulders. Persecution, trials, and hard times may be in the offing. But oh, how rich be the sailing and life at sea with the Son and Skipper.

On a previous occasion, we discussed three profound events in the life of a believer: being saved and born again into the Son, water baptism as a public confirmation of what be in your heart — your conviction that the Son be the Savior of the world — and the baptism of the Holy

Ghost of Truth. Each deepens our relationship with Skipper and His Son.

In John 17, we find the Son, on the night before the cross, praying in extraordinary detail about how this relationship be lived out.

He reminds us that we were Skipper's before the world began — a profound declaration, confirmed in Jeremiah 1:5 and Psalm 139:13-16. In John 17, Jesus declares:

> We be protected by the power of Jesus' name: the name given by the Father.
> We be one with Skipper and with the Son.
> We carry Skipper's words in our hearts.
> Our true citizenship be in heaven, not on earth.
> The Son ***desires*** to live in complete union with every believer.
> That Skipper be in the Son and the Son be in us — Skipper himself be in us.

That the love Skipper has for His own Son now lives inside of us. And because the love of the Father for the Son lives in us, we can love others the way the Son and Father love others.

This be life with and in Skipper — up close. Inside the believer. Joined to our spirit. Creating. Renewing. Restoring. Making whole. This be believers sailing forth in the same Spirit, authority, and power Jesus carried when he calmed storms, walked on water, healed the sick, fed the poor, and raised the dead. And this, mates, be our calling and commission.

Now picture two ships sitting in the same harbor.

Both be seaworthy. Both have been inspected, registered, and launched from the yard. Both fly the same colors. From the dock, they look identical. But when the wind pipes up, the sails of one fill and the sails of the other hang limp. One moves, the other sits. One departs for vast lands to deliver the good news of Jesus. The other remains in port and becomes the "watering hole" for local congregants who speak of sailing but never sail.

This, mates, be the difference between being saved and being filled with the Holy Ghost of Truth. Both believers, both vessels, re-christened by Skipper and part of His fleet. But only one constantly, consistently moves with the wind.

In Acts 1:1, Luke writes that in his first account, he recorded all that Jesus *began* to do and to teach. Began. Not finished. The Son healed the sick, raised the dead, cast out demons, preached good news to the poor, and set the oppressed free — and then He handed this commission to His crew. "As the Father has sent me, I am sending you" (John 20:21). "Greater works than these shall ye do, because I go to the Father" (John 14:12). The fleet be not meant to remain anchored in harbor, not by a long shot with a bow cannon.

In the Harbor… But Not Yet Under Sail

We know the thief on the cross were saved. In Luke 23:43, the Son says, *"Truly I tell you, today ye will be with me in paradise."* Mark this word, pirates and lubbers alike: those who die in the Son and slip their cable to sail for paradise be the lucky ones.

The Eleven were saved before the crucifixion. The Son said of them, *"I have not lost one of those ye gave me."* (John 18:9) No doubt from the time of the crucifixion until the outpouring of the Holy Ghost of Truth at Pentecost, some believers died without ever being born of the Holy Ghost of Truth — saved, registered, in the harbor, but sails never filled. And still the promise of paradise be their final port.

In John 20:22, the Son breathed on the disciples and said, "Receive the Holy Spirit." But the wind didn't come — not fully — until fifty days later at Pentecost. "Stay in the city until ye have been clothed with power from on high." (Luke 24:49)

When Pentecost finally came, the Scripture says the sound fell upon the crew like a rushing, violent wind filling the whole house (Acts 2:2). This be like a white squall building from off the horizon, rushing across water— but in a good way. This squall of wind turned the fleet upside down. From old ships to new. From worn sails to fresh, from that moment on, those newly christened vessels in the fleet rode the wind of the Holy Spirit of Truth.

Two Baptisms: The Wedding and the Wedding Night

The Son makes clear that water baptism and Spirit baptism be two distinct events.

"John baptized with water, but in a few days ye will be baptized with the Holy Spirit." (Acts 1:5)

Water baptism be the wedding — the public declaration, the visible commission, the colors nailed to the mast for all to see. Holy Spirit baptism be the wedding night — our intimate union with the Son filling us. The consummation of the covenant. Two becoming one. At our new birth, we go into the Son. At our Spirit baptism, He comes into us. This be a holy moment, a sacred surrendering of our flesh and spirit to Him.

For many, receiving the Holy Ghost of Truth be such an intimate event that it best be enjoyed in private. The vulnerability, the joy, the tears, the warmth — it be much the same as the intimacy of a wedding night between a bride and groom. And rightly so, for Christ Jesus be our groom and we his bride. Yes, mates, in this context even pirates — male and female — be the bride of Jesus. Aye, even the roughest, most barnacled, least-bathed old salt among us be His bride. Hold fast to that image, ye yellow-livered scurvy dogs, and try not to lose your lunch.

The Great Commission in Matthew 28:19 points to both: "Go and make disciples of all nations, baptizing them in the name of the **Father** and of the **Son** and of the **Holy Spirit**." **The Father**: saved by grace through faith into the Son. **The Son**: water baptism, the outward seal confirming our trust in Jesus. **Holy Spirit**: filled with the fullness of His Spirit, faith, authority, power, all the fruits of the Spirit Jesus enjoyed when He went about doing good.

Baptize. Ask. Receive.

The instructions of the Son on this be straightforward:

> "Go! Baptize them into the Holy Spirit."
> "Receive the Holy Spirit."
> "Your Father in heaven will give the Holy Spirit to those who ask him!" (Luke 11:13)

Notice the three actions: baptize, ask, receive. A prize must be taken to be yours. Ye can stand on the dock with your arms at your sides while someone tries to hand ye the lines, but until ye reach out and take hold of your end, the rope dangles.

In Acts 8:15-17, we see this played out. Peter and John arrive to find new believers — lubbers who be saved— but have not yet received the Holy Ghost of Truth. "The

Holy Spirit had not yet come on any of them; they had simply been baptized in the name of the Lord Jesus." So Peter and John placed their hands on them, prayed, and they received the Holy Ghost of Truth.

Saved, yes, but their sails were not yet filled with wind.

Later, in Acts 19:2, Paul encounters another group of believers and asks directly: "Did ye receive the Holy Spirit when ye believed?" Their answer hit like a bucket of cold water. "No, we have not even heard that there is a Holy Spirit."

They had been sailing under their own power, doing the work of the Son in their own strength. Faithful, sincere, obedient — but without the wind that makes a long-distance voyage not only possible but enjoyable. The difference between the wind of the Holy Ghost of Truth and saved-but-working-in-our-own-strength be the difference between a ship sailing and a crew rowing. Both might bring the craft to port — but by thunder, the crew of the canoe-gig-longboat be tuckered out, sunburned, and in no condition to tell anyone about the voyage by the time they stumble up the wharf.

The Breath of Skipper Changes Everything

Being ***filled*** with the Holy Ghost of Truth be not a gentle suggestion. He be the wind of Skipper — the same *pneuma*, the same breath, the same *ruach* that moved over the waters at creation (Genesis 1:2), that turned timid and fearful disciples into Torah-thumping preachers and teachers who chastised the religious leaders of their day. The same explosive Spirit that the Son promised would guide His people into all truth and raise the dead, heal the sick, and send demons skedaddling (John 16:13)

Paul, simply by being filled with the Holy Ghost of Truth and speaking with power, poured out the Spirit on those who heard him. (Acts 11:15-17) The wind were so present in Paul that it spilled over into the room. This be what a fully rigged, Spirit-filled vessel looks like — not just slicing across seas, but generating a great wake that causes other crew to turn and stare.

"By the power of the Holy Spirit, may the God of hope ***fill ye*** with all ***joy*** and ***peace*** as ye ***trust*** in him, so that ye may ***overflow with hope***" (Romans 15:13).

Fill ye so that ye overflow. That be not a trickle. That be a vessel running with the wind at full sail, spray off the bow, colors flying. If ye not be filled with joy, peace, trust in Skipper, and hope for the visions He give ye, then it may very well be 'cause ye be not filled.

There be some not-so-good-news naysayers among the brethren who say suffering be part of the believer's life. And to be sure, all will go through hard times. Only Jesus and Paul both make clear: this suffering comes from folks, not the Father. Persecution comes from sailing under the colours of Christ and sticking by His words. Some claim sickness be a teacher sent by Skipper — that

Skipper uses pain to instruct us in matters He couldn't impart any other way.

But the Son promised to send the Holy Ghost of Truth that He ***might*** *"Teach ye all things"* (John 14:26). If Skipper can only teach us through sickness and suffering, then the Holy Ghost of Truth be insufficient. Or else, we be so empty of His Spirit of Truth, that we get learning elsewhere.

Some say we should be thankful Skipper doesn't always say yes to healing. That we should be thankful we be not promised health, wealth, and happiness. That we should delight in trouble so we might take up our cross, die to self, and trudge on through life until we reach heaven. Somehow, this message ought to warm the cockles of our hearts and leave us jubilant that Jesus came, suffered, and died to save us.

But if health, joy, and provision be not guaranteed — if all Skipper's promises be *maybe* or *not in this life* — then what do we make of the words of Paul who said, "My God shall supply all your need according to His riches in glory" (Philippians 4:19)? What do we do with Isaiah's words — and Peter's confirming statement — that by His stripes we be healed (Isaiah 53:5)? Either the beating, flogging, lashes, and pummeling he suffered before the cross healed us or didn't. The Son said plainly that He came so we "may have life and have it abundantly" (John 10:10). Not abundantly in heaven one day — abundantly now. Jesus ***is*** the prosperity Gospel.

If His Holy Ghost of Truth testifies to this truth, will the Father not give us all things necessary for life?

Look at how often the Son told His crew to ask the Father. "Ask, and it will be given to you; seek, and you will find; knock, and the door will be opened." (Matthew 7:7) "Whatever you ask in my name, I will do it." (John 14:13) "If you remain in me and my words remain in you, ask whatever you wish, and it will be done for you." (John 15:7) "Ask and you will receive, that your joy may be full." (John 16:24) "Your Father in heaven will give the ***Holy Spirit*** to those who ask him." (Luke 11:13)

Ask. Seek. Knock. Ask in His name. Ask and receive. The Son said it over and again, in different rooms, on different days, to the same crew — because He wanted it lodged deep in their hold. He wanted his crew filled with His Holy Spirit of Truth.

A Leaking Hull and the Need for Daily Filling

Here be something every honest sailor knows: a vessel in the water leaks. Not catastrophically, perhaps. But the sea finds its way in through every seam, every imperfection, every place where the wood has worked in a storm. Keeping a vessel afloat requires constant attention: pumping, caulking, bailing where needed. Any sailor who tells you his vessel doesn't leak be either a blind bilge rat or in the shipyard.

In the same way, "be filled with the Spirit" (Ephesians 5:18) be not a onetime event. It be a command — present tense, ongoing. Our earthly vessels leak. The pressures of sailing, living, and luffing while trying to make port drain us of His Spirit. This be why we return daily to the Word, to prayer, to fellowship, and most of all to asking to be filled afresh. Not because we lack His Holy Ghost of Truth — but because we need His Spirit quickened in us. We need the daily flushing out of every work of the flesh, every offense, every sin, everything that causes us to leak. If the Spirit of Skipper lives in you, ye be not in the realm of the flesh but be in the realm of the Spirit (Romans 8:9).

Ripe or Rotten, Fruit Gives the Lay of Things

How can ye tell if ye be filled with the Holy Ghost of Truth? The same way ye can tell which way the wind be blowing — look for evidence. Wind leaves whitecaps, waves, and spray. No wind? Dead calm. No Spirit? Dead works.

The fruit of the Spirit is ***love, joy, peace, forbearance, kindness, goodness, faithfulness, gentleness,*** and ***self-control*** (Galatians 5:22-23). We ought to add to this ***Skipper's faith*** (Mark 11:22), for it be the faith of Skipper working in our spirit that empowers us to believe for what we cannot see.

If what we be speaking is the inevitability of lack, loss, and suffering: if we be living with apathy, sadness, and expecting that by our own efforts we can keep from sinning, we need a fresh filling of the Holy Ghost of Truth.

Unity in the body also comes by the Spirit. "We were all baptized by one Spirit to form one body — and we were all given the one Spirit to drink" (1 Corinthians 12:13). When ships in a fleet share the same wind, they sail together. When some keep their sails furled while others run before the wind, the fleet separates. This be why we see divisions — not because the Son be divided, but because not every vessel in the harbor be filled with His wind.

Like Stede Bonnet, a man can have a fine-looking vessel, sailing under the right colors, and filled with a hearty crew — but still lose everything because he were pretending and posturing.

The End of the Matter

If ye cannot recall being baptized with water, get baptized. Hold the wedding.

If ye cannot recall receiving the Holy Ghost of Truth — if the wind has never filled your sails in a way ye could point to and say, "There, that were the moment" — then find a quiet place, drop to your knees, and ask to be filled. Ask for the wind. Skipper gives the Holy Ghost of Truth to those who ask (Luke 11:13). Wait for the wind. Ye will know when it comes. Your innards may grow warm. Tears may flow. From your lips, words in a new language will come forth.

Then enjoy the honeymoon night. Aye, there be nothing more glorious to a believer than to be filled with the Spirit of Jesus. Ye in Him. Him in ye. Get the full package.

Warning to Crew: The effort to realign others with the words, actions, and promises of the Son and Skipper be sure to bring persecution and pushback, you may lay to that. The Son suffered the same from the religious leaders of His day. They hated Him because He healed on the Sabbath. But healing be not work for Jesus. For Jesus, healing be pure joy. And He wants us to share in this joy.

So, aye, those who practice religion — working in the flesh to do what the Son has already done — will throw rocks. It be how religion reacts when confronted with grace. But truth be truth. Jesus commanded us to go and do as He went. We can only do that through the fullness of Him.

Ask your Father in heaven for ***His Holy Spirit***.

Pirate Facts

Mates served as apprentices to the Ship's Master, Boatswain, Carpenter, and Gunner, and took care of the fitting out of the vessel. Mates examine whether the ship be sufficiently provided with ropes, pulleys, sails, and all the other rigging necessary for the voyage. Mates also take care of hoisting the anchor. During a passage, the crew checks the tackle once a day. If a mate observes anything amiss, he or she reports this to the Ship's Master. Arriving at a port, shipmates help repair the cables and anchors and attend to the management of the sails, yards, and mooring of the ship.

Chapter Six

How to Read Skipper's Code: Wreckers, False Lights, and the One True Chart

Scripture Reading for Truth, Clarity, and Spiritual Insight

There are stories told in the Bahamas of how skippers sailing along the eastern edge of the Abacos kept watch through the night for lights to the west.

During the 18th and 19th centuries, impoverished islanders discovered that a ship on a reef be a vessel

> *"A verse read in context be a reliable chart. A verse ripped out of context be a counterfeit — a lantern on a reef."*

worthy of pillaging and plundering. But winds, waves, and storms — the happenstance of nature — only rarely delivered. So in storms, when visibility collapsed, and captains were already uncertain of their latitude and longitude, wreckers would walk the coastline — and those who dared — the reefs, swinging lanterns. Some tied smaller lights to cattle that bobbed and drifted in the dark, mimicking the steady light of a safe channel or a friendly harbor — a scheme that required the full cooperation of the cattle, who, to their credit, asked no questions. A captain, trusting what he saw, would correct his course toward the light, even if the chart suggested otherwise.

And the reef would find the ship's keel. Once stuck, waves and relentless pounding would break the ship's spine, and she would split, dumping crew and cargo onto hard coral that, on calmer days, would be plucked and taken ashore. These wreckers sometimes saved crew and passengers, but not always. When wealth matters more than life, discretion be cast aside.

The wreckers didn't need to rewrite the charts. They only needed to offer something no chart could show: a light that looked trustworthy in the dark.

This be what happens to those who receive Scripture secondhand without ever taking the time to read it. They trust the words of teachers and speakers, assuming these "lights" be grounded on solid soil. And when we place our confidence in the light of others, rather than the light of Jesus, our faith be at risk of grounding.

In his first letter to Timothy, Paul speaks of Hymenaeus and Alexander, whose faith were described as "shipwrecked." He writes: holding on to faith and a good conscience, which some have rejected and so have suffered shipwreck with regard to the faith. Among them are Hymenaeus and Alexander, whom I have handed over to Satan to be taught not to blaspheme. (1 Timothy 1:19–20)

Shiver me timbers — those be not men who stumbled onto a reef in a storm — they sailed straight onto it in fair weather, with a good chart in hand, because they stopped trusting it.

The Bible be unlike any other book. It be living and active (Hebrews 4:12), and it does not simply inform the mind — it transforms the spirit. But that transformation depends on how we approach it. Careless reading leads us onto shoals, sandbars, and reefs. Destruction be not absolute. Often, by setting our anchor in deeper water, we can kedge off. But these momentary groundings can be avoided by sticking to the charts. Distorted readings lead to false doctrine. And in a world full of voices all claiming to speak truth, learning to read Scripture well be not optional. It be essential seamanship.

The prudent skipper doesn't critique teachers, preachers, and leaders. Rather, he simply studies the charts and comes to know the sea — the color of the bottom, the churn of currents — until he can discern false sightings from the real truth found in Skipper's word. He be an old salt, not a landlubber standing wide-eyed on the dock, taking the word of any scurvy dog who claims to know these waters. When we sit under teaching, we judge whether it be true: if it aligns with Skipper's word. Weigh what be questionable, and hold fast to what be good. (1 Thessalonians 5:21)

Start with Prayer, Not a Pen

Before ye open your Bible, open your heart.

A wise captain never sets sail without first checking conditions: the wind, the sky, and the urgency to depart. All factors into when to cast off. There be no point in setting a course if the risk of weather — or pirates and wreckers — will cost ye crew, cargo, and ship. Paul understood this well when he prepared to sail to Rome. Approaching the late and dangerous sailing season off the coast of Crete, he warned those in charge that the voyage ahead would bring damage and great loss — not only to cargo and ship, but to their lives. They ignored him, sailed into a storm of hurricane force, and wrecked on the island of Malta. Paul tried to tell them, he did. (Acts 27:9–10) They ignored him, which historians note be a fairly consistent response to good advice delivered at inconvenient moments.

The Holy Spirit be the wind in our sails. He be the teacher. Jesus promised that the Spirit would guide us into all truth (John 16:13). The Holy Spirit comforts us and comes alongside us as our Counselor and Helper, the one Jesus promised the Father would send in His name (John 14:16, 26). And a comfortable crew be a happy crew. That means the most important thing ye bring to any passage be not a commentary or a concordance, but a posture of humility and dependence on the wind: the Spirit of Skipper in our hearts.

Ask the Spirit to illuminate the text. Ask Him to guard ye from your own assumptions. The person who prays before they read will often see more than the scholar who has studied the passage for years. Why? Because those who ask the Spirit to lead and guide have asked the One who drew the chart, marked the coordinates, and wrote its words to help them plot their course. That be no dead reckoning — that be the Author Himself standing at the helm.

Context Is the Chart

Every passage of Scripture lives inside a story. It has a before and an after. It belongs to a chapter, a book, a testament, and an overarching narrative that runs from Genesis to Revelation. Before ye settle on what a verse means, ask: What be happening around it? Who be speaking? Who be listening? What has just happened, and what comes next?

Pulling a verse out of context be one of the most common — and dangerous — habits in Bible reading. It be, in fact, the oldest trick in the wrecker's tool kit. This be exactly the strategy the devil used when he tempted Jesus in the wilderness: taking a word from the Lord and twisting it just enough to wreck Jesus' faith. But it didn't work. Jesus knew the chart — drew the chart. Blast ye, the devil — he got every word right and still ran his prize aground. Jesus also knew that a sentence lifted from its surroundings can be made to say almost anything. When ye hear a verse, and it appeals to the flesh, emotions, or intellect, belay that. Stop and check it. Read that verse in its original setting to see if that were its intended meaning, and in what context it were first spoken. This helps us differentiate lights on shore from lights on reefs.

Keep every passage in its home waters. A verse read in context be a reliable chart. A verse ripped out of context be a counterfeit, a lantern on a reef.

Cultural Context: Use It, Don't Live in It

Understanding the world in which a passage were written adds value and flavor, but that be intellectual knowledge, not spiritual understanding. Knowing the geography, the customs, the political climate, and the daily life of the people helps us enter the narrative and feel its weight.

A seasoned sailor — a true sea dog — understands the tides, the local currents, and the seasonal winds of the region. This adds richness to the passage, but it be only head knowledge. A sailor who spends all his time studying the water and never leaves port has learned a great deal and been nowhere. Sailing requires that we leave the familiar in order to venture out into the unknown. Test the teaching. If a speaker or teacher spends an inordinate amount of time talking about culture, circumstances, the attitude and actions of the characters in the text, but struggles to bring fresh spiritual meaning to the verse, this may suggest that he spends most of his time sailing in familiar waters. Like Peter, he be still waiting for Jesus to command him to "put out into deep water." Smart as paint, perhaps, but still tied to the dock.

The stage be not the story. Characters carry the theme and purpose of a narrative, not the props. If a teacher spends most of their time on historical background and very little time on spiritual meaning, pay attention. Rich cultural detail with thin spiritual application can leave us well-informed but spiritually adrift. The goal of

Scripture be not to take us back to ancient Israel. It be to bring Skipper's eternal truth into our lives today.

Watch for Repeated Words and Themes

Skipper be intentional. When a word, image, or theme appears more than once in a passage — or echoes across multiple books — that repetition be a signal worth following. When Jesus says "Truly, truly" in John's Gospel, He be essentially saying: Avast. This matters. Lean in.

Think of repetition as a lighthouse. Flash once; we look. Flash twice; we take a bearing. This be the value of repetition: it demands that we mark the verse and acknowledge that the Author of the chart wants to warn, bless, or command us. Rush past two-light flashes, and ye may come to regret it, and no mistake.

Go Back to the Source Language

Charts be translated from ancient languages, some of which be no longer spoken. The same be true of the Bible ye read. We may not know Greek or Hebrew, but with a good concordance, we can quickly gain a broad understanding of a word's original meaning, purpose, and context in Scripture.

The New Testament were written in Greek. The Old Testament in Hebrew and Aramaic. When a word feels unclear or seems out of step with the rest of the passage, look it up. Discover how that word be used elsewhere in Scripture. The same Greek word translated *peace* in one verse might carry the deeper sense of wholeness or completeness, and that changes everything about what ye be reading. Here be one example: study all the ways the word "dogs" be used in Scripture. Jesus referred to Gentiles as "dogs" — not pets, but unclean, as in not holy and chosen like the Jews. Later in Revelation, Jesus says "dogs" remain outside the New Jerusalem. Be Jesus declaring that all animals but dogs gain entry? In Revelation, there be a long list of animals seen in heaven. The source language gets to the root of a word's meaning.

The writers of Scripture chose their words with care. Skipper inspired every one of them. The source language be where those choices live. Don't settle for a translation of a translation when the original be right there in your pocket. A good hand knows the ropes; he doesn't hand the wheel to someone who's only read about sailing.

Follow the Breadcrumbs

Following breadcrumbs be different from checking a word for clarity. This be tracking a word or image across the whole of Scripture to see what it meant, how it grew, and where it leads. Rather than studying to find the meaning of a word that leaves us confused or unsure, in this case, a word in Scripture leads us on a journey of enjoyment and enlightenment.

Take the word *lamb*. Follow it from Abel's offering in Genesis, through the Passover in Egypt, through the sacrificial system of the Law, through Isaiah 53, into John the Baptist's declaration at the Jordan — *"Behold, the Lamb of God"* — and finally to the throne room in Revelation where the Lamb receives all glory and honor.

What ye find be not a collection of scattered references. It be a river of meaning running through the entire story of Skipper, arriving at Christ. Follow it long enough, and ye will understand why John the Baptist said what he said, why it electrified the people standing in the water with him, and why the vision in Revelation makes the saints fall on their faces.

Look at all the ways water, oil, light, sea — these words be used in Skipper's word. Some definitions be literal, but many carry spiritual meaning.

By thunder, this kind of breadcrumb study be where the Bible stops feeling like a library of separate books and begins to feel like one voice: one where the Author speaks to us. It be often in these moments that the Holy Spirit speaks something fresh and specific, not just to your mind, but to your spirit.

Evaluate in Community

No sailor worth his salt navigates entirely alone. A second set of eyes on the charts has saved more ships than any single captain's confidence ever did.

The Bible were not written to be read in isolation, and it were not meant to be interpreted alone. Throughout history, the most dangerous doctrinal errors have come from individuals who cut themselves off from the correction of others and followed their own reading wherever it led: sometimes straight onto the rocks, sometimes over the edge of the known world.

Paul calls this reading and studying and listening with "itching ears" — hearing what we want to confirm as true, even when it be false. Three sheets to the wind and convinced they be sailing straight.

When ye arrive at an interpretation, bring it to the crew. Look for people who know Skipper's Word deeply enough to find the passages that confirm or challenge what ye've found. And be discerning here: memorization alone be not evidence of spiritual understanding. Satan knows the Bible. He quoted it to Jesus in the wilderness and got every word right. But that reef wrecker intentionally misapplied its meaning, flying false colors from the moment he opened his mouth. What ye be looking for be not a concordance in human form, but someone who knows the Spirit behind the Word well enough to recognize when an interpretation rings true, or when it be a black spot on the chart.

The body of Christ be one of Skipper's primary instruments for keeping us honest and keeping us on course.

Use Commentaries as a Last Resort

There be an old pirate joke buried in the word: commentators be often just common taters — dressed-up potatoes with a French accent sailing under a Spanish flag. The humor points to something true.

Commentaries can be useful. But reach for them last, not first.

Before ye seek insight from others, do the harder and more rewarding work of sitting with the Lord in the passage. Pray. Wrestle. Look at the context, the repeated themes, and the source language. Let the Holy Spirit have the first word. Think of it as digging for treasure ye know be under sand. Ye can buy a map and dig it up, or follow Skipper's Spirit and let Him lead ye to a prize meant just for ye. When ye uncover something ye worked and waited and prayed to receive, it be *yours* — a truth pieces of eight could never buy. Skipper hides things for us to find; that be for His joy and ours.

If ye reach for a commentary, look for those that dig into the Greek and Hebrew: ones that open up the meaning of specific words rather than simply retelling the story in more sophisticated language. These can be genuinely useful additions to your study.

Better to let Jesus, through His Holy Spirit, be your teacher than some bilge rat author who may or may not be on a first-name basis with Skipper, and whose theological credentials consist primarily of endorsements from dead writers.

Hold Your Interpretations Humbly

Even the best navigator has been wrong about a position.

Ye will not get every passage right. Neither will your pastor. Neither will the most celebrated theologian. This be not a weakness; it be part of how Skipper reveals His mysteries to those who ask.

Jesus promised to give us greater revelation, to remind us of all He taught, and to disclose what had been hidden since the foundation of the world. That means our understanding today be meant to deepen tomorrow. There will be moments when something we held as true turns out to be incomplete, or, if we have relied on the word of man, entirely incorrect. If we be genuinely led by the Spirit, those moments should be few. But they will come, so be on guard. And when they do, the humble sailor adjusts the heading, while the proud one insists the chart be wrong and sails on into the reef.

Pride be the great enemy of wisdom. This were the error of the Pharisees. They were certain, beyond instruction and insight, of how the Messiah would come and be recognized. Yellow-livered in their faith and iron-fisted in their pride, they missed seeing Him when Jesus stood before them. Become rooted in the revelation ye receive, but stay open to the Spirit's ability to shift, refine, or redirect ye to His fuller truth. The goal be not to master Scripture. The goal be to be mastered by it.

Come to every passage asking not only, "What does this mean?" but, "Lord, what be ye saying to me today through this?" That posture keeps the Word alive and keeps ye teachable for whatever He has next.

And when a passage resists ye — when its meaning won't become clear no matter how long ye sit with it — take that to Him too. Ask for understanding. Like the disciples, there will be times when He withholds greater insight because we cannot yet receive it. Jesus said as much: *"I have much more to say to you, more than you can now bear."* (John 16:12) This be not rejection. If the desire to understand be burning in ye, it be because He placed it there. He wants ye to come to Him, keep asking, keep seeking, because He wants ye to know.

So be comfortable wrestling with a passage. Expect Jesus to wrestle with ye. That wrestling be fellowship. It be part of the deep, pure joy that only comes from time in Skipper's Word — a joy the world cannot manufacture or take away, and no storm can wash it overboard. Hold fast to that.

Skipper's Nature

Finally, align what ye know of Skipper's character over the passage. Verify that your understanding of the text matches His nature, His history, and His word. His word be His nature. His nature reflects His word. Skipper cannot violate who He be. He be truth. His word be truth. This be the final test of His meaning.

The waters around the Abacos and Grand Bahama be, by any measure, among the most treacherous — and most storied — in the entire Caribbean. Conservative estimates place the total number of shipwrecks across the Bahamian archipelago somewhere between 3,000 and 5,000, with a single focused survey of the northern Abaco region alone identifying nearly 600 wrecks, the oldest dating to 1657. The majority ran aground on reefs and island shores, not open water. And historians believe that for some, it were no accident. A lantern swinging on the coast, patient and deliberate, held by someone who understood exactly what a desperate captain would do when he spotted what looked like safe harbor in the dark. The wreckers didn't build the reefs. They didn't summon the storms. They simply knew that a man who trusts a false light will wreck his vessel just as surely as a man who trusts a faulty chart. The reef be not the cause. False lights and our failure to trust the one pure chart — Skipper's word — be what wrecks our faith.

Stick to the chart. Test all lights. And when in doubt, follow the one true light.

Pirate Facts

A grog maid serves beverages in a pub or tavern. Grog maids also act as the public image of the establishment, contributing to its reputation. For example, drinks like Bloody Mary, Shirley Temple, and Margarita be named after grog maids.

Chapter Seven

The Wealth of Wisdom

Cargo in the Ship's Hold

There be a particular kind of despair that comes not from one catastrophic storm, but from a slow drift into the doldrums.

No single wave capsized the vessel. No reef tore out the hull. No storm drove her onto a shoal. The ship just drifted — which, as any experienced sailor will tell ye, be a slower and more embarrassing catastrophe. A little off course here. A degree or two in the wrong direction there. Days passed. Then weeks. And somewhere along the way, the captain looked up from the deck and realized he had no idea of his long and lat. No wind in his sails. No chart

> *The most treacherous waters in the world can be navigated safely by a wise captain in a modest vessel. The finest ship ever built can be wrecked by a fool with good weather and a following wind."*

that seemed to match the surrounding waters. Dead in the water and lost.

Maybe that be where ye be right now.

Worried? Anxious? Struggling with depression? In broken relationships — or several? Overworked? Underpaid? Can't pay your bills? Feeling lost and stuck with no port in sight?

Here be the word for ye today: Skipper has this.

All ye need for peace, provision, health, and wholeness be the Holy Spirit of Jesus living in ye, revealing the treasures found in Skipper's Word. Jesus didn't drift. He didn't lose sleep over tomorrow — and He doesn't want ye losing sleep either.

He be speaking to ye right now:

> *"Peace I leave with you; my peace I give you. Do not let your hearts be troubled and do not be afraid."* (John 14:27)

> *"In this world you will have trouble. But take heart! I have overcome the world."* (John 16:33)

> *"Come to me, all you who are weary and burdened, and I will give you rest."* (Matthew 11:28)

The storm does not have the final say. He does.

The Most Valuable Cargo in Any Hold

Solomon, the wisest man who ever lived, spent the opening chapters of Proverbs doing one thing: trying to convince his son — and anyone else who would listen — that wisdom be the most valuable thing a vessel can carry.

Not gold. Not silver. Not the favor of kings, nor the admiration of crowds. Wisdom.

> *"Blessed is the one who finds wisdom, the one who gains understanding. For wisdom is more profitable than silver and yields better returns than gold."* (Proverbs 3:13-14)

> *"Wisdom is supreme; though it costs you everything, get wisdom and understanding. Esteem Wisdom, and it will exalt you. Embrace Wisdom, and it will honor you."* (Proverbs 4:7-8)

Every seasoned captain knows this. The most treacherous waters in the world can be navigated safely by a wise captain in a modest vessel. And the finest ship ever built can be wrecked by a fool with good weather, a following wind, and complete confidence in his own judgment — which be the most dangerous cargo a vessel can carry. The difference be not the vessel. It be what the captain carries between his ears and in his heart.

Skipper's Wisdom in Jesus provides a rich and fruitful life — not a life without hardship, but a life with the knowledge and discernment to navigate hardship without being destroyed by it. Respect for the Lord be the beginning of that wisdom: instruction, understanding, insight, a disciplined and prudent life, a course that be just and fair. (Proverbs 1:2-4)

Not sure which port to make for, which heading to take, or how to keep provisions on the ship? With the Holy Spirit's guidance, ye can tap into Skipper's wisdom and receive clarity, direction, and confidence in every leg of the voyage.

> Jesus says: *"Ask. Seek. Knock. My Father in heaven desires to give good things to those who ask Him."* (Matthew 7:11)

How to Use Skipper's Word for Today's Voyage

If ye feel overwhelmed by anxiety and despair, what follows be not a list of pleasant thoughts. It be a chart — drawn by the hand of Skipper, tested across thousands of years of human seafaring, and as reliable today as the day it were written.

Open your Bible. Read these passages slowly. Ask the Holy Spirit to show ye which verse be for ye today, for your specific problem, in this exact moment. He will speak if ye ask. And when ye get a word from the Lord, stand on it. Don't let the waves talk ye out of it. Trust that Skipper will honor His word and do for ye what He has said.

Blessings: The Wisdom that Guides Your Course

> *"Do not forget God's teachings. Keep his commands in your heart. They will prolong your life for many years and bring you prosperity."* (Proverbs 3:1-2)

> *"With God's Wisdom you will win favor and a good name in the sight of God and men."* (Proverbs 3:4)

> *"God's Wisdom will bring health to your body and nourishment to your bones."* (Proverbs 3:8)

> *"God's Wisdom fills your hold to overflowing and provides all you need for a rich life."* (Proverbs 3:10)

> *"Wisdom is a tree of life to those who rest on her branches."* (Proverbs 3:18)

> *"Wisdom is life to those who find her and health to a man's body."* (Proverbs 4:22)

"Make level paths for your feet and take only ways that are firm. Do not swerve to the left or right. Then you will walk in the good way." (Proverbs 4:26-27)

Promises Charted by the Hand of Skipper

"Whoever listens to the words of the Lord will live in safety. They will be at ease and without fear of harm." (Proverbs 1:33)

"Wisdom holds victory in store for the upright. Wisdom is a shield to those whose walk is blameless. Wisdom guards the course of the just and protects the way of His faithful ones." (Proverbs 2:7-8)

"With Wisdom you will understand what is right, just, and fair. You will find every good path. Wisdom will enter your heart. Knowledge will be pleasant to your soul. Discretion will protect you. Understanding will guard you." (Proverbs 2:9-11)

"In all your ways acknowledge God, and He will make your paths straight." (Proverbs 3:6)

"When you lie down, you will not be afraid; when you lie down, your sleep will be sweet." (Proverbs 3:24)

"Have no fear of disaster or the ruin that overtakes others, for the Lord is your confidence. He will keep your foot from being snared." (Proverbs 3:25-26)

"The Lord blesses the home of the righteous. The wise inherit honor." (Proverbs 3:33-35)

Warnings: Reefs Marked on the Chart

"Fear of the Lord. Turn when He rebukes, and He will pour out His heart to you. He will make His thoughts known to you." (Proverbs 1:29-30)

"Do not be wise in your own eyes. Instead, fear the Lord and shun evil." (Proverbs 3:7)

"The Lord disciplines those He loves, as a father disciplines the son he delights in." (Proverbs 3:12)

"Above all else, guard your heart, for it is the wellspring of life." (Proverbs 4:23)

Wisdom and Instruction from Your Captain

"Attain wisdom and instruction, understanding and insight. Acquire a disciplined and prudent life. Do what is right, just, and fair." (Proverbs 1:2-4)

"The naïve gain knowledge and discretion, and increase in learning. Listen, learn, and gain discernment and guidance for understanding proverbs and parables, for sayings and riddles of the wise." (Proverbs 1:5-6)

"If you accept His words and store up His commands in your heart; if you turn your ear to wisdom and apply your heart to understanding… then you will understand the fear of the Lord and find the knowledge of God." (Proverbs 2:1-5)

"The Lord gives wisdom; from His mouth come knowledge and understanding." (Proverbs 2:6)

"Let love and faithfulness never leave you. Bind them around your neck. Write them on the tablets of your heart." (Proverbs 3:3)

"Blessed is the one who finds wisdom, the one who gains understanding. For wisdom is more profitable than silver and yields better returns than gold." (Proverbs 3:13-14)

"Preserve sound judgment and discernment. Do not let them out of your sight. They will be life to you and an ornament of grace around your neck. Then you will go on your way in safety, and your foot will not stumble." (Proverbs 3:21-23)

"Wisdom is supreme; though it costs you everything, get wisdom and understanding. Esteem Wisdom, and it will exalt you. Embrace Wisdom, and it will honor you." (Proverbs 4:7-8)

"The path of the righteous is like the first gleam of dawn, shining ever brighter until the full light of day." (Proverbs 4:18)

Guidance for Life: Standing His Orders

"Honor the Lord with your wealth, with the firstfruits of all the works of your hands." (Proverbs 3:9)

"Let your eyes look straight ahead and your gaze directly before you." (Proverbs 4:25)

Get Into the Word and Let His Word Get Into Ye

Get into Jesus. Get into Skipper's Word. Get Jesus in ye. Get Skipper's Word in ye.

Before long, ye will see evidence that His Word be working — not just filling your head, but steadying your hull, adjusting your heading, and guiding ye out of the fog and into open water.

Still not convinced that Skipper wants ye well, prosperous, and sailing in the abundant life He designed for ye? Then consider this: Skipper sent Jesus to show exactly how much He loves ye.

"Jesus' name is the Word of God." (Revelation 19:13)

> *"In the beginning was the Word, and the Word was with God, and the Word was God."* (John 1:1)

> *"The Word became flesh and made his dwelling among us — full of grace and truth."* (John 1:14)

Jesus be not too good to be true. He be simply true to ye — if ye will turn to Him, take His hand, and let Him set your course.

The treasure be real. The charts be trustworthy. The wind be ready.

Raise your sails.

Pirate Facts

Wenches be young women or female servants taken aboard a ship as cargo who, through choice or force, decide to remain as crew. Though women be not generally welcome aboard, wenches serve at the pleasure of the captain and may sometimes outperform the (mostly) male crew. They may also serve with and replace the ship's cook, at which point they become a galley wench.

Chapter Eight

Why Ye Be Not Prospering

What Skipper Really Says About Success

Two merchant captains set sail from the same port on the same morning, bound for the same destination, in vessels of equal size and equal age.

One arrived wealthy. His hold were full. His crew were loyal. His reputation in every port along the route had grown with each voyage until merchants would wait weeks for his ship rather than sail with someone else. He weren't lucky. He weren't born with a better vessel. He

> *"Diligence, obedience, and generosity be not the price of Skipper's love. They be the sails that catch the wind of His blessing."*

worked his routes with discipline, honored every agreement he made, and gave generously at every port — to crew, to merchants, to those who had nothing. Word spread. Doors opened. The tide seemed to favor him everywhere he sailed.

The other captain arrived broke. Not because the sea were against him. Not because the winds failed him. He cut corners on maintenance until the hull leaked. He broke agreements when a better deal appeared. He held his cargo with a tight fist and gave nothing away, convinced that generosity were a luxury he couldn't afford. His crew quietly abandoned him at every port — which, given his pay scale, they considered a reasonable career decision. His reputation arrived in harbors before he did — and not in a good way.

Same sea. Same wind. Same starting point. Completely different outcomes.

This be not a parable about luck or talent, or divine favoritism. It be a picture of what Skipper has been saying since Solomon first put stylus to papyrus in the book of Proverbs: the way ye sail determines where ye end up. And there be principles — Skipper's principles — that govern the waters of prosperity as surely as the tides govern the sea.

If ye be not prospering, the question worth asking be not "Why has Skipper abandoned me?" but "Am I sailing by His charts?"

What Prosperity Actually Be

Before we go further, let's agree on what we're talking about — because the world's definition of prosperity and Skipper's definition be sailing in opposite directions.

The world says prosperity be the size of your hold. How much have ye accumulated? How full the treasure chest looks at the end of the voyage.

Skipper says prosperity be the condition of your whole vessel — hull, rigging, crew, cargo, and course. It be peace that holds steady in a squall. It be relationships that don't fracture under pressure. It be health, purpose, provision, and the kind of sleep Proverbs 3:24 promises to the person whose life be rightly ordered: *"When you lie down, you will not be afraid; when you lie down, your sleep will be sweet."*

True prosperity, as Scripture presents it, be a holistic life — purpose, provision, peace, and the promise of something far greater than this voyage can contain.

Earthly abundance, when it comes, be a foretaste. The real treasure be eternal.

With that settled, here be the three principles Skipper's Word names again and again as the difference between a vessel that arrives full and one that limps into port empty.

Diligence: Work the Rigging

There be a particular kind of sailor that every experienced captain recognizes immediately. He be always on deck when it matters. His lines be coiled before he be asked. When the wind shifts at three in the morning, he be already adjusting the sails before the captain has rolled out of his bunk. He does not wait to be told what needs doing. He sees it, and he does it.

This be the sailor who ends up with his own ship.

Skipper has never been ambiguous about the relationship between diligence and prosperity. Solomon says it plainly, three different ways, so there be no confusion:

> *"He who has a slack hand becomes poor, but the hand of the diligent makes rich."* (Proverbs 10:4)

> *"The plans of the diligent lead surely to plenty."* (Proverbs 21:5)

> *"The soul of the diligent shall be made rich."*
> (Proverbs 13:4)

Notice what be not said here. Solomon does not say that a talented hand makes one rich. He does not say the well-connected or the fortunate, or those born into the right family. He says the diligent hand. The one that shows up. The one who plans, executes, and keeps working when others have gone below decks.

Skipper honors hard work. He built it into the fabric of creation. Adam were given a garden to tend before the fall; work were not a curse, it were a calling. The curse made it harder. Christ redeems even that.

So before ye ask Skipper why the winds haven't favored ye, ask yourself honestly: Am I working the rigging? Not frantically, not anxiously — but purposefully, consistently, with the kind of steady effort that builds something over time. Diligence be not desperation. It be faithfulness applied to daily work.

Where can ye be more diligent — in your work, your relationships, your spiritual life? The answer to that question may be the answer to the prosperity question.

Obedience: Sail the Charted Course

Every experienced navigator knows that there be waters ye simply do not enter. Not because someone be trying to keep ye from adventure, but because the reef be real. The shoal be there whether ye believe in it or not. The chart marks it because someone ran aground there before ye, and the mark on the chart be their gift to every captain who comes after.

Skipper's commands work the same way.

They be not arbitrary restrictions. They be navigational markings drawn by the One who made the sea — who knows every reef, every current, every hidden danger in the waters of human life. When He says, "sail here, not there," He be not limiting your voyage. He be protecting it.

Leviticus 26:3-5 makes the connection explicit: obedience brings rain, abundant harvests, and safety. Deuteronomy 28:1-11 goes further: *"If you diligently obey… you will be set high above all nations"* — blessed in the city and in the field, blessed when ye come in and when ye go out, your enemies routing before ye, your storehouses overflowing, everything ye put your hand to succeeding.

> And Joshua 1:7-8 ties it directly to the Word: *"Be careful to obey all the law… do not turn from it to the right or to the left, that you may be successful wherever you go. Keep this Book of the Law always on your lips; meditate on it day and night, so that you may be careful to do everything written in it. Then you will be prosperous and successful."*

The chart be the Word. Meditating on it day and night be not a religious exercise — it be seamanship. It be internalizing the navigational markings so thoroughly that when the fog rolls in and the stars disappear, your hands still know which way to steer.

Disobedience be not freedom. It be sailing without charts into waters ye don't know, in the dark, at speed. The reef doesn't care how confident ye be.

Commit to walking in Skipper's ways. Not because obedience earns His love — ye already have that. But because obedience opens the door to His blessings, and those doors be worth walking through.

Generosity: Give Away What Ye Cannot Keep

Here be the one that sinks most captains.

There be a deep, irrational fear that lives in the hold of every human heart — the fear that if we give something away, we will not have enough. That generosity be a leak in the hull. That every coin released be a coin lost.

Scripture says the exact opposite be true.

> *"The generous soul will be made rich, and he who waters will also be watered."* (Proverbs 11:25)

> *"Give, and it will be given to you: good measure, pressed down, shaken together, and running over."* (Luke 6:38)

The image in Luke be of a merchant at the market, filling your sack with grain — not just to the brim, but shaking it down to settle it, pressing it, then piling more on top until it overflows. This be what Skipper says happens when ye give. Not a trickle back. An overflow.

The reason be theological as much as practical. Generosity aligns your heart with Skipper's heart. Skipper be by nature a giver. *"He who did not spare His own Son, but gave Him up for us all — how will He not also, along with Him, freely give us all things?"* (Romans 8:32) The whole story of Scripture be the story of a Skipper who gives extravagantly, sacrificially, without guarantee of return.

When ye give, ye step into that current. Ye begin to sail with the nature of Skipper rather than against it.

The captain who hoards his cargo, refuses to pay his crew fairly, and gives nothing to the ports he visits will find those ports closed to him over time. The captain who gives to his crew, to the poor, to the work of Skipper, will find that the sea seems to open before him in ways he cannot fully explain.

Embrace generosity not as a religious obligation but as a way of life. Trust that Skipper will meet and exceed your needs. He has said so in terms ye cannot misread.

Skipper's Provision: More Than a Full Hold and Filled Heart

Here be what gets missed in every worldly conversation about prosperity: Skipper's provision be not primarily about the size of your treasure chest.

> *"The Lord is my shepherd; I shall not want."* (Psalm 23:1)

> *"Ask, and it will be given to you; seek, and you will find; knock, and it will be opened to you."* (Matthew 7:7)

The shepherd in Psalm 23 does not promise his sheep a palace. He promises them green pastures, still waters, a table in the presence of enemies, and a cup that runs over. He promises that goodness and mercy will follow them all the days of their lives. This be provision that goes far deeper than coin — it be the kind of provision that means ye be never truly without, never truly lost, never truly abandoned, no matter what the weather looks like from the deck.

Skipper's provision includes peace when the sea be rough and purpose when the course feels unclear. Relationships that hold when the storm hits. Health that goes beyond the physical. A sense of meaning that the world's prosperity — all its gold and silver and status — can never manufacture.

Seek Skipper's provision in every area of your life. Not just the financial ledger. The whole vessel — hull, crew, compass, and course. He supplies all your needs. (Philippians 4:19) Trust that.

Eternal Prosperity: The Port That Never Closes

Every earthly voyage ends. The most prosperous captain who ever lived eventually handed over his charts for the last time and stepped off the deck for good.

But here be the extraordinary promise of the gospel: the best be not behind ye. It be not even in the most successful leg of your current voyage. The best be ahead — in a port that never closes, where the weather be always fair, and the treasure be beyond calculation.

> *"God will wipe away every tear from their eyes; there shall be no more death, nor sorrow, nor crying."* (Revelation 21:4)

> *"He who did not spare His own Son… how shall He not with Him also freely give us all things?"* (Romans 8:32)

> *"I will bless you… and you shall be a blessing."* (Genesis 12:2)

Earthly blessings — the fruit of diligence, obedience, and generosity — be real and worth pursuing. But they be a foretaste. A glimpse through the spyglass at what awaits at the final port. The abundant life Jesus promised be not something that begins in eternity. It begins now, on this voyage, in these waters. But it does not end here.

Live with an eternal perspective. Use your earthly blessings to glorify Skipper and bless others. Let the treasure ye accumulate serve the voyage, not become the voyage. Because the voyage itself be leading somewhere, and where it leads makes everything else worth it.

Be Ye Sailing Skipper's Course?

Before ye leave this section, sit with these questions honestly.

Be ye diligent — working your rigging, showing up, planning, and executing with faithfulness? Or be ye waiting for favorable winds that ye haven't earned yet?

Be ye obedient — sailing the charted course, honoring Skipper's navigational markings even when they seem to take ye the long way around? Or be ye cutting across waters that He has marked as dangerous?

Be ye generous — giving freely from what Skipper has placed in your hold, trusting that the current of His nature will bring it back and then some? Or be ye hoarding, afraid that an open hand means an empty hold?

The charts be clear. The course be laid out. The wind of the Holy Spirit be ready.

The only question be whether ye be willing to raise your sails and sail it.

> *"Diligence, obedience, and generosity be not the price of Skipper's love. They be the sails that catch the wind of His blessing."*

Pirate Facts

These be not real monkeys, but they do remain hunched over while working, respond poorly to sudden loud noises, and oftentimes smell like monkeys. The distinction, at close range, be largely academic.

Chapter Nine

Your Vessel

The Authority of the Governed Soul

François L'Olonnais knew how to take a vessel.

Born Jean-David Nau, a servant boy from Brittany, he made his way to the Caribbean and became the most feared buccaneer of his age. Fléau des Espagnols — the Flail of the Spaniards — commanded ships, men, and entire coastlines through sheer, savage force. His reputation were so monstrous that Spanish prisoners chose death in battle over surrender to his cutlass — a choice historians note be among the more efficiently made decisions of the era. He raided Cuba. He sacked

> *"The question has never been whether Skipper has enough rope to reach from heaven to earth. The question always be whether the crew be willing to be the rope He made us to be."*

Maracaibo. He plundered the Gulf of Honduras. No port felt safe. No captain felt ready.

He governed everything the sea offered — but he could not govern himself. And when he met his maker, there were no galleons to flee to, no crew to command, no cutlass to save him. Deep in the jungles of Panama, the Flail of the Spaniards, met his end at the hands of Darien Indians — torn limb from limb while screaming terribly. That matter concluded, he were burned to ash — which, by any measure, be a poor performance review for a man who had spent thirty years terrifying everyone else.

An ungoverned vessel does not sail forever. It founders. And sometimes dies a gruesome death.

L'Olonnais spent his life seizing vessels that were never his to command. But our Skipper, our Maker, approaches governance differently. He builds vessels in His image — men and women — and places us at the helm. Not a prize taken by force. A commission given by design.

From the beginning, Skipper did something that still startles many and inspires some. He made man in His image; then He handed us the helm. We be commanded to drive the ship: to sail with His authority. And while Skipper seems confident that we be up to the task, for many, standing the helm and commanding a vessel be a terrifying thought. We'd rather defer to Skipper and declare that He be in charge. Teach that His ways be mysterious. Preach that Skipper's will may be for us to suffer in health, poverty, and broken relationships in this life, so we can learn from Him and draw nearer to Him. To take responsibility for the vessel requires that we work, learn, and be accountable.

The Son went about ministering to others. Ministering, not giving 'em a tongue lashing. Many there be among the crew who invert Skipper's grace and mercy, turning His love into lessons administered by a taskmaster seemingly bent on breaking our backs and spirits. Beat down, we be tempted to "let go and let Skip" take back the helm — to give wind, waves, rudder, and keel free rein to drive our vessel wherever it may. Somehow, someway, we believe Skipper will magically make all things right: if not in this life, in the next.

Aye, this be the attitude of a naïve swab of no good use to the crew and ill prepared to guide a vessel to its home port.

> *"Be fruitful and multiply, fill the earth and* ***subdue*** *it, have* ***dominion,"*** (Genesis 1:28).

Subdue. Dominion. These be our instructions. Commands that sound like work. Directives that place the outcome in our hands. The Hebrew *kabash* — subdue — means to press under, to bring into subjection. *Radah* — dominion — means to rule, to govern, to reign over. Skipper were not simply suggesting we command our vessel. He were issuing a commission. He were naming us the captain and handing over the charts.

But notice what dominion be not. It be not force. It be not coercion. It be not white-knuckled control through pressure and striving.

Dominion be the **authority to decide direction.**

We do not push the swells. We read them. We set headings, watch clouds, feel the wind on our faces, and catch the smells of a distant land. This be the life of a sailor at sea. This be the life of a Believer reigning on earth.

Skipper works miracles, aye. But most days, He works through us. Wind, waves, and currents may bring a ship into harbor, but the expectation be that a man or woman stands at the helm, steering the craft into the harbor. Skipper governs through spiritual laws, through natural and economic laws. He entrusts humans with stewardship and expects us to use these laws for our good and the good of others.

He gave us the vessel, our bodies. He gives us the charts: His word. He gave us the commission: His authority to act on His behalf. The question always be the same: Will we take the helm and use all laws to reach port?

What it Means to "Wait Upon the Lord"

Religion teaches that maturity means waiting upon the Lord. Aye, we be called to wait, but waiting be action, not sitting, resting, nodding off. To "wait" be to serve Skipper, to wait in the manner of an attendant looking for a chance to please his master. Faith means hoping. We *wait* through motivation, inspiration, and gaining more knowledge of His will. We *wait* through circumstances and change outcomes, making good of bad, better what were lost. We *wait* and gain clarity by taking action, steering a course, and moving. A ship adrift be at the mercy of nature. One under sail can be governed. And if it be clear the course be wrong, the crew can come about.

Skipper promised His people a land of promise. He promised to go before them. He promised He would fight for them. But He commanded them to take the land, to walk the land, to possess the land.

Believers share in all the promises. From Abraham to the Son, all Skipper's promises be "yes" and "let it be done." But promises without action be no better than a Sunday sermon empty of Skipper's power. The crowds were amazed at the Son's preaching because He spoke as one with authority. How be authority spoken? What does authority sound like? Perhaps what they heard were the Son speaking as if He believed His words. He spoke with conviction, with the confidence that if He said a thing, it would be. He spoke, "Yes. Let it be done." And He *expected* it would be done.

The Rope That Reaches From Heaven

On a ship, there be no such thing as rope. The moment a rope be pressed into service aboard a vessel, it becomes something new. It earns a name and a function. The same be true of the Believer.

The Hebrew word for *wait* be *qavah*. It be the word Isaiah reaches for when he writes the most quoted promise in all of prophetic literature: *"They that wait upon the Lord shall renew their strength"* (Isaiah 40:31). *Qavah* be rope-making. It be the ancient, deliberate act of twisting individual strands together — each one too weak to hold anything on its own — until what ye hold in your hands can bear the weight of a ship. That be what Skipper had in mind when He said, *wait.* He commands us to *twist ourselves into* ***Him****. To build each other up strand by strand until we can bear the load of one another.* And here be where the theology becomes the vessel's own rigging.

Walk aboard any working vessel — schooner, brigantine, or sloop — and ye will find every rope be assigned a task. This be *qavah.* When ye bind yourself to the Lord — twist yourself into Him, strand by strand — ye be *made into something strong enough to serve.* Consider how the Son placed His commands in the hands of His crew.

The Halyard. *"Go into all the world and preach the gospel"* (Mark 16:15). The halyard hauls the sail to the top of the mast. It be the line that helps your vessel catch the wind — Skipper's Spirit. The halyard doesn't catch the wind, but it allows our sails to spread, billow, and be filled. Coiled on deck, nice and tidy, the ship's halyard grows mold from dampness, and the vessel goes nowhere. When the Believer opens his mouth and declares the gospel, he be hauling up the sail. He be sending the vessel forward in faith.

The Sheet. *"Teaching them to observe all things that I have commanded you,"* (Matthew 28:20). If the halyard raises the sail, the sheet *trims* it. The sheet be the line that the sailor holds in his hand, constantly adjusting, tightening, easing, angling the sail to the wind's direction. A halyard without a sheet produces a sail flogging out of control, full of noise and fury. Teaching be the work of a sheet. Teaching takes the message and pulls it tight or lets it fly. The teacher who *qavahs* upon the Lord reads the wind — Skipper's Spirit — and makes slight adjustments to gain maximum power. We be not tasked with merely delivering information. We be commanded to trim the sail so that every soul aboard catches the same wind and moves as one.

Cords for Binding. *"Lay hands on the sick, and they shall recover"* (Mark 16:18).

Every ship carries cord for binding. The moment a crewman goes down — a fall from the rigging, a wound from battle — cords were torn or cut and pressed into service on the spot.

A sailor knows that the smallest rope on any vessel be a thread. And it be the thread where everything begins. In the Son's day, women spun linen thread by hand. They pulled raw flax fiber from the plant, twisting it onto a drop spindle, strand by strand, until it became yarn, then cloth, then strips cut and pressed into service wherever the body needed tending. Pirates tell yarns — elaborate tales that string together multiple moments of humor, entertainment — and occasionally a nautical truth. A humorous pirate yarn can keep the crew in stitches. But alas, I have needled this point enough.

Aboard ship, these strips served two purposes above all others. They received the newborn — wrapping the infant tight, binding it into life. And they received the dead — wound close around the body and sealed. Birth. Death. The same thread serves both. The Son, an infant, arrived wrapped in one. The Son, the Messiah, left the others behind Him in the tomb — folded, empty, finished.

And now He places such sacred cloth in the hands of His crew. So, *"Lay hands on the sick, and they shall recover."*

Of all the lines aboard this vessel, this may be the most needed by the crew, and the least deployed. And why? Because too many in the fleet do not believe the Son's words. As to why some trust doctors and medicine, but not the Son's words, be a question each mate must answer.

The Dock Line. *"Cast out demons"* (Mark 16:17). The dock line secures what has been brought into port against the forces that would drag it back out to sea. Our authority to cast out and take what the Son has secured for us be our dock line. *"What ye bind on earth be bound in heaven. What ye loose on earth be loosed in heaven,"* (Matthew 18:18). Our binding and loosening keeps us attached to our firm foundation — the Rock of the Son — and guards the fleet from marauders who seek to steal.

The Lifeline. *"Freely ye have received, freely give,"* (Matthew 10:8). The lifeline runs along the rail of the vessel. Its single purpose be to keep the crew aboard: to prevent a man from going over the side in heavy seas. Acts of mercy, generosity, giving to the poor, visiting the sick and in prison, our presence in the suffering — these be lifelines. The Believer who acts as a lifeline — who *goes* when it be inconvenient, who *gives* when it comes at great sacrifice, who *sits* with someone in the storm of their life — be the lifeline. And like this rope that runs around the edge of the vessel, we may never know how many took hold of a lifeline a moment before being swept into the sea.

Ye Be The Rope

Here be what *qavah* promises. *"Those who wait upon the Lord shall renew their strength"* (Isaiah 40:31). The sailor who *qavahs* hands over his weakness and receives strength in the Lord. But notice the verbs that follow: *they shall mount up... they shall run... they shall walk.* This be not passive sitting. This be the most active thing a human being can do. The Son said, *"I have given you authority"* (Luke 10:19). Past tense. Already done. Already deployed.

The question has never been whether Skipper has enough rope to reach from heaven to earth and accomplish His will. The question always be whether the crew be *willing* to be the rope He made us to be.

Choose Before Ye Feel Ready

> *"I have set before you life and death, blessing and cursing. Therefore, choose life,"* (Deuteronomy 30:19).

Heaven and earth as witnesses. This be legal language. This be a court in session. Skipper be not presenting options for emotional consideration. He be assigning responsibility. He be saying: the options have already been placed before ye. Nothing here waits on heaven's decision. The only unresolved element be **your participation.**

A captain does not always wait until the weather feels favorable before setting his heading. He sets the heading and sails with the weather there is.

Choice be **jurisdiction.** Choice be the place of a commissioned authority. Choice decides direction before conditions agree. When ye wake up in the storm and declare, *"I will not be ruled by fear today,"* ye be not denying the storm's power over your spirit. Ye be assigning it a lower rank. Ye be telling fear: *ye may be present, but ye will not be in charge.*

That be governance. And governance always brings peace.

Keep Your Mind Stayed on the Son

> *"Ye will keep him in perfect peace whose mind be stayed on You,"* (Isaiah 26:3).

Stayed implies placement. Intention. Fixed in position. A mind that be anchored in Skipper's truth has a specific heading and be certain of arrival. A stayed mind continues to look at the acts of the Son, believes His words, and carries out His commands. Wind and rain, sun and heat, regardless of the elements, a stayed mind remains on watch. This be perseverance. This be a rope Skipper can depend upon: a rope that will not fray from chafing, but will always perform its task.

Guard Your Heart

> *"Guard your heart with all diligence, for out of it flow the issues of life"* (Proverbs 4:23).

The word *issues* in Hebrew means outflows — boundaries, directions, borders. Life does not merely happen to the heart. **Life flows from it.**

Every experienced sailor knows that what gets into the ship's bilge stays unless pumped out. Too much in, and she rides heavy — and may even sink. A compromised hull lets in water slowly. No alarm sounds at first. The ship still moves. The crew works the bilge pumps. But below the waterline, unseen in the darkness, seams be opening and filling the vessel.

Our hearts be the containers, and whatever we allow in will eventually overflow into our lives. Fear replayed becomes fear expected. Disappointment rehearsed becomes disappointment anticipated. Offense nursed becomes offense as identity. Guarding the heart means deciding what gets into the ship's hold. The question be simple: What will we allow to travel in our hearts to the next port? Because whatever we carry will be deposited when we step ashore.

Take Thoughts Captive

> *"Take every thought captive to obey the Son,"* (2 Corinthians 10:5).

A thought be a visitor. It knocks. It presents its case. It offers its narrative. But it only gains power when it be **agreed with.**

The old naval term for an enemy vessel boarded and seized be a **prize.** The prize crew takes control of the captured ship and redirects it. That be precisely the image Scripture be using. A thought that goes unexamined becomes a belief. A belief becomes a conclusion. A conclusion shapes identity. And identity determines declaration.

This be why the chain of captivity matters:

> *Thought → Agreement → Belief → Conclusion → Identity → Declaration → Life.*

Take every thought captive. Examine it; name it; measure it against Skipper's word. And if it be of the enemy, enforce Skipper's will over the captive and make them obedient to the Son. This means we march captives to the Son and ask Him to overlay His word on each combatant — that through His Holy Spirit, He interrogates the prisoner and commands it to obey Skipper's word.

Because declarations spoken carry weight, we must arrest thoughts as soon as they appear on deck. Ship them to the brig. Give the Son charge over them. And only when they be obedient to Him do we permit them to speak.

Words That Hold Authority

> The Son said to the fig tree: *"Let no fruit grow on ye."* He said to the storm: *"Peace. Be still."* He told his crew, *"Whoever says to this mountain, 'Be lifted up and thrown into the sea,' and does not doubt in his heart... it will be done,"* (Mark 11:23).

Notice what He did not say. He did not say *pray about the mountain.* He instructed us to *talk to the mountain. The mountain be listening.* Why? Because Skipper made it. The mountain knows the source of its creation. It heard a word from the Creator, and it existed. The mountain still listens for further instructions from the Creator. But here, the Son does something remarkable. He delegates Skipper's authority to believers.

When the Son spoke to storms, He spoke on earth words from heaven. Now He has commanded us to do the same. When He commissioned the crew with authority in Luke 10:19 — *"I have given you authority"* — He gave it. Past tense. His authority be ours to carry. But carrying authority be not the same thing as exercising authority. The Son never doubted that the words He spoke would manifest the intended outcome. He knew His Father's words would accomplish their purpose.

> *"Death and life be in the power of the tongue"* (Proverbs 18:21). Skipper said: *Subdue creation. Have dominion over it.* Paul said: *We reign in life through the Son* (Romans 5:17).

By enforcing His will — through action when called, through declaration when His Holy Ghost of Truth speaks — we bring heaven to earth and do the works the Son did, and greater. *"Those who receive abundance of grace and of the gift of righteousness will reign in life through the One, the Son"* (Romans 5:17).

Reign. Govern. Act justly; make right what be broken. Be righteous as He be righteous; make new what be missing. Show mercy. Give grace in abundance. These be the commands we've received from our Captain.

L'Olonnais captained himself. And this man, who served only himself, died by the same savagery he lived by — torn apart in a jungle, remembered only for his brutality. The Son said it plainly: those who live by the sword die by the sword. But the Believer who reigns under Skipper's authority governs not by the sword, but by the Word. And that Word brings life. To us. To those we command. To every port we enter. Govern wisely.

Pirate Facts

Although technically not a rank, a swab be a sailor who mops the decks using the swab. Thus becoming a "swabbie." The term has come to describe someone who be not held in high regard by the commander and crew.

Chapter Ten

The Making of a Miracle

Every seasoned sailor knows that the sea changes as ye leave the shallows behind.

> *"He be not too grand for the mud. He be not too holy for the mess."*

Close to shore, the water be bright, transparent, and manageable. Ye can see the bottom. Ye know roughly what lies beneath. The risks be real but readable: sandbars, rocks, and the occasional rogue current. But as ye sail further out, the color of the water darkens. The bottom disappears. The depth beneath your keel becomes something ye can no longer measure with a simple line and a lead weight. The sea becomes something vast and alive and beyond your full comprehension — and yet somehow, impossibly, more beautiful the deeper it gets.

This be how Jesus moves through the Gospels.

He does not arrive and immediately raise the dead. He begins close to shore — a fever here, a withered hand there, ten lepers cleansed on a dusty road. Manageable miracles. Miracles ye could almost explain away if ye were determined to. But with each passing chapter, He sails further out. The water darkens. The depth beneath His words becomes something no one can measure. And by the time ye reach the tomb of Lazarus — four days dead, stone rolled across the entrance, the stench of finality in the air — ye be in waters so deep that only one thing be left to do.

Watch. And believe.

Close to Shore — Authority Over the Body

The first miracles of Jesus be not small. But they be, in the language of the sea, coastal waters. He be establishing something before He takes us further out. He be letting the crew get their sea legs before the deep water comes.

Consider the blind man at Bethsaida. (Mark 8:22-26) Friends bring him. He doesn't even find Jesus himself; he be led to Him. Jesus takes him by the hand, leads him outside the village, and does something unusual:

He heals him in two stages. First touch — the man sees people, but blurry, like trees walking. Second touch — sharp, clear, complete.

Why two stages? Because Jesus be showing us something about how He works. Not always in a single flash. Sometimes in a process. Sometimes clarity comes in stages, and the first partial sight be not a failure; it be the first touch on the way to the second. If ye be in that place right now, where things be becoming clearer but not yet clear, ye be not forgotten. Ye be between the two touches.

Then there be the paralyzed man at the pool of Bethesda. (John 5:8) Thirty-eight years. Thirty-eight years of lying there, watching others get into the water before him, watching healing happen to everyone except him. And Jesus walks up and asks what might be the most pointed question in the Gospels: *"Do you want to get well?"*

It sounds almost cruel. Of course he wants to get well. But Jesus be asking something deeper. Because after thirty-eight years, the identity of the sick man can become more comfortable than the terrifying freedom of the well man. Some of us have been lying by our pool so long that we have forgotten what it felt like to stand.

> *"Get up. Pick up your mat and walk."*

And he did.

Then the ten lepers on the road. (Luke 17:11-19) They stand at a distance — as lepers must — and cry out: *"Jesus, Master, have pity on us!"* And Jesus does something remarkable. He doesn't touch them. He doesn't pray over them on the spot. He simply says, *"Go, show yourselves to the priests."* And it were as they went — as they obeyed, as they walked in faith before any visible evidence had appeared — that they were cleansed.

Ten set out. Ten were healed. But only one turned back. Only one fell at Jesus' feet and gave thanks.

> *"Where are the other nine?"*

The miracle had reached all ten. But only one let the miracle reach his heart.

These early works establish something foundational: Jesus has authority over physical suffering. The body be not beyond His reach. No disease too chronic, no blindness too long, no paralysis too deep. He be the Lord of the shoreline. But He be not finished. He be taking us further out.

Into Deeper Water — Authority Over Body and Spirit

A sailor who has only seen coastal waters thinks he knows the sea. He doesn't. Not until he has been days from any shore, with nothing around him but horizon in every direction, does he begin to understand what the sea actually be.

This be where Jesus takes us next.

The man lowered through the roof. (Mark 2:1-12) Four friends — desperate, creative, and unwilling to be stopped by a crowd — tear open the roof of a house and lower their paralyzed friend down on a mat to the feet of Jesus. The room were packed. The religious leaders were watching. And Jesus looks at the man lying at His feet and says something that shocks everyone in the room:

> *"Son, your sins are forgiven."*

Not "be healed." Not "get up." Sins forgiven.

The religious leaders immediately recognize what Jesus be claiming. Only Skipper can forgive sins. They accuse Him of blasphemy in their hearts. And Jesus — who knows exactly what they were thinking — looks at them and says: *"Which is easier: to say to this paralyzed man, 'Your sins are forgiven,' or to say, 'Get up, take your mat and walk'? But I want you to know that the Son of Man has authority on earth to forgive sins."*

Then He heals the man.

He does the visible miracle to prove the invisible one had already happened. The healed body were evidence that the soul had already been reached. Jesus be not just a healer of flesh. He be the only One in the universe with the authority to reach into the deepest, most broken place in a human being — the place where guilt and shame and separation from Skipper have taken root — and say: forgiven.

Then the man born blind. (John 9:1-7) The disciples, steeped in the theology of their day, ask whose sin caused the blindness — the man's, or his parents'. Jesus cuts the question off at the knees. *"Neither. This happened so that the works of God might be displayed in him."*

Then He spits in the dirt, makes mud, spreads it on the man's eyes, and tells him to wash in the Pool of Siloam.

Mud. Spit. The Creator of the universe, who spoke light into existence with a word, gets His hands dirty to heal one blind man on an ordinary afternoon. There be something about this miracle that should stop us cold. He be not too grand for the mud. He be not too holy for the mess. He made the first man from dust, and He be not above kneeling in it again.

And then — the woman with the issue of blood. (Luke 8:43-48) Twelve years of hemorrhaging. Twelve years of being considered ceremonially unclean. Twelve years of being untouchable, excluded, invisible. She doesn't ask for an appointment. She doesn't cry out from a distance. She simply decides: if I can just touch the edge of His garment, I will be healed.

She reaches. She touches. And immediately the bleeding stops.

Jesus stops abruptly. *"Who touched me?"* The disciples be stunned. People be pressing in from every side. But Jesus knows that power has gone out from Him. He waits. The woman, trembling, falls at His feet and tells Him everything.

And He calls her *"Daughter."*

Not "woman." Not "ye there." Daughter. He gives her back her dignity, her belonging, her name in the family of Skipper — publicly, in front of everyone who had spent twelve years pretending she didn't exist.

We be now far from shore. The water be dark and vast. But Jesus be not finished. He be taking us somewhere that will change everything.

Faith: The Wind That Fills These Sails

Before we go into deep water, we need to pause and feel the wind.

Because woven through every one of these miracles be a thread that Jesus keeps pulling on, keeps pointing to, keeps calling out by name. Not the miracles themselves: the faith that preceded them.

Blind Bartimaeus sits by the road outside Jericho, hearing the crowd approach. (Mark 10:46-52) Someone tells him Jesus of Nazareth be passing. And Bartimaeus, blind and begging, begins to shout: *"Son of David, have mercy on me!"*

The crowd tells him to be quiet. He shouts louder.

"Son of David, have mercy on me!"

This be not a polite request. This be a man throwing his whole weight against the door. This be a man who has decided that this moment — this single moment in an otherwise ordinary afternoon — be his moment, and no crowd be going to take it from him. Jesus stops. Calls him over. And says: *"What do you want me to do for you?"*

"Rabbi, I want to see."

"Go. Your faith has healed you."

And the woman with the issue of blood — her faith were so quiet it were nearly invisible. No shouting, no crowds, no dramatic appeal. Just a hand reaching through a crush of people to touch the hem of a garment. But Jesus noticed. He always notices.

Faith be the wind. Expectations be the sails. Without wind, sails hang limp. With it, the vessel moves in ways that defy explanation. Ye do not need great faith — Bartimaeus had nothing but his voice and his desperation. Ye do not need visible faith — the woman had nothing but a silent, determined reach in a crowd. Ye need only faith that be aimed at Jesus.

That be enough. It has always been enough.

Into the Deep — Authority Over Death Itself

And now we leave the last sight of land behind.

The widow of Nain. (Luke 7:11-17) A funeral procession coming out of the city gates: a mother, already a widow, following the body of her only son. She has lost everything. There be no safety net, no provision, no future that she can see. Just a body on a bier and the long, empty years stretching ahead.

Jesus sees her. And the Gospel says something that should anchor every soul reading this:

He had compassion on her.

Not on the crowd. Not on the spectacle. On her. He saw one grieving mother in a crowd, and something moved in Him that could not stay still.

He touches the bier. The bearers stop. And He says: *"Young man, I say to you, get up."*

The dead man sat up and began to speak.

The crowd, Luke tells us, were filled with awe and praised Skipper: *"A great prophet has appeared among us. God has come to help his people."*

They didn't fully know yet how right they were.

And then — Lazarus. (John 11:1-44) This be the deep water. This be the place where every natural explanation runs out, and ye be left with nothing but the question Jesus be about to answer with His own hands.

Mary and Martha send word to Jesus: *"Lord, the one you love is sick."* And Jesus — who loves Lazarus, who loves this family — deliberately waits. Two days. He does not rush. He does not hurry to the shore. He waits until the moment be exactly right, until the miracle He be about to perform cannot be explained away, cannot be diminished, cannot be attributed to anything less than what it actually be.

By the time He arrives, Lazarus has been in the tomb four days. Four days in the heat of the Middle East. This were not a coma. This were not a misdiagnosis. Martha says it herself: *"Lord, there will be a bad odor, for he has been there four days."*

Jesus weeps.

The shortest verse in the Bible. The most profound. The Son of Skipper — who knows full well what He be about to do, who could in this moment see past the tomb to the breakfast He will share with Lazarus in a few minutes — weeps with the sisters, anyway. Because their grief be real. Because their loss be real. Because compassion be not diminished by foreknowledge.

He stands before the sealed tomb and commands: *"Take away the stone."*

Martha hesitates. Jesus holds her gaze: *"Did I not tell you that if you believe, you will see the glory of God?"*

The stone be moved.

Jesus lifts His eyes to heaven, prays aloud — *"Father, I thank you that you have heard me"* — and then turns to face the dark mouth of the tomb and calls out in a loud voice:

> *"Lazarus, come out!"*

And the dead man, still wrapped in his burial cloths, walks out of the tomb.

We be in fathomless water now. There be no bottom. No chart covers these depths. This be the sea that swallows everything ye thought ye knew and gives back something greater in return.

The Final Port — He Walks Out of His Own Tomb

But Lazarus would die again. The widow's son would die again. Every person Jesus healed on those dusty roads and in those crowded houses would eventually face the tomb.

The miracles were signs. They were pointing somewhere. And where they pointed were to a tomb outside Jerusalem, sealed with a Roman stone and guarded by Roman soldiers, on a Sunday morning when the whole world thought the story were over.

> *"I am the resurrection and the life. The one who believes in me will live, even though they die; and whoever lives by believing in me will never die."* (John 11:25-26)

Jesus said these words standing outside the tomb of His friend. He meant them for Lazarus. He meant them for Martha. He meant them for every person who would ever stand at a graveside and feel the cold weight of finality.

And then He proved them — not by raising someone else, but by dying Himself, going into the dark, and walking out the other side under His own power.

No one carried Him out on a bier. No one rolled away the stone for Him. No one called His name from outside. The guards were there. The seal were in place. Death did everything death knows how to do.

And on the third morning, the stone were already rolled away when the women arrived. Not to let Jesus out — He were already gone. But to let the witnesses in, so they could see for themselves what were no longer there.

The grave clothes were neatly folded. The tomb were empty. The sea of death — crossed.

> *"He who did not spare His own Son, but gave Him up for us all — how will He not also, along with Him, freely give us all things?"* (Romans 8:32)

The Same Power Lives in Your Hold

This be not ancient history sealed in a book. This be the living inheritance of every person who has received the Spirit of Christ.

The same power that opened blind eyes be available to ye. The same authority that silenced twelve years of hemorrhaging flows through the prayers of Spirit-filled believers. The same compassion that stopped a funeral procession outside the gates of Nain moves in the heart of every follower of Christ who has learned to see with His eyes.

And the same resurrection power — the power that walked Lazarus out of his tomb and Jesus out of His — be the power that raised Christ from the dead and now lives in ye. (Romans 8:11)

Ye be not a spectator to these miracles. Ye be a vessel commissioned to carry them into every dark harbor, every grief-soaked shoreline, every place where someone has sealed a stone over their hope and given up waiting.

Jesus' miracles be a progression. But they be not finished. They be still unfolding — in your life, through your hands, in the name of the One who sailed into the deepest water of all and came back.

No situation be beyond His reach. No storm be beyond His authority. No tomb — not even the one ye think be sealed forever — be beyond His voice.

He be the resurrection and the life.

That be not a doctrine. It be a Person.

And He be standing outside your tomb right now, calling your name.

"Come out."

Pirate Facts

The Sailing Master navigates and sails the ship. He or she directs the course and looks after the maps and instruments, compass, and such necessary fer navigation. Since charts of the waters where we sail be often inaccurate — or in some instances just don't exist, having been drawn by someone who had apparently never visited the area in question — this position requires someone with sharp eyes and who knows ter look out fer danger beneath the ship's keel. Being a Sailing Master means first sailing with the Master. Make it your mark to master the work put upon ye.

Chapter Eleven

Set Your Anchor in the Right Port

By 1596, Sir Francis Drake had nothing left to prove. He were the most feared English sailor alive — a farmer's son from Plymouth who had made himself a legend. He plundered Spanish galleons up and down the Spanish Main, circumnavigated the globe aboard the *Golden Hind*, and became the first Englishman ever to do so. He raided Spanish colonies from Hispaniola

> *"Down to Davy Jones' Locker he went. Down. Not up."*

to Florida, sacked the port of Vigo, and personally handed Queen Elizabeth I enough treasure to make her crown shine brighter. She called him her pirate and knighted him on the deck of his own ship, which gives a whole new meaning to the word "decked him."

The Spanish put a price on his head — and still, not a scurvy dog among them could bring him down. He survived it all — every storm, every engagement, every close call.

At fifty-five, convinced there still be treasure in the offing, Drake set sail for the Spanish Main one final time. Smart as paint most days, his instincts told him a prize be there. But sword, cannon, and musket never got the chance to prove him wrong.

The fever slipped him the black spot. Somewhere off the coast of Portobelo, Panama, Sir Francis Drake — privateer, national hero, the Queen's own pirate — took sick and died. They buried him at sea in a lead coffin, dropping him into the very waters he had spent his life conquering.

Down to Davy Jones' Locker he went. Down. Not up.

And that be precisely where Drake's story crosses our bow — because Paul tells us something all mates, lubbers, and swabbies alike, need to hear. *"Set your minds on things above"* (Colossians 3:2), for a day of dead reckoning awaits all. Drake never set his anchor in the right port. Aye, it were hardly ever set for long anyplace.

And, by thunder, where ye set the flukes often determines the life ye lead, live, and leave.

The Anchor That Holds

Here be what the Good Book says 'bout setting your anchor, and it be worth reading slow:

"Have *this hope* as an anchor for the soul, firm and secure." (Hebrews 6:19) What hope, what anchor? Why, an anchor for the soul. Firm. Secure. An anchor that grips the bottom tighter when the current, wind, and wave be attempting to pull the vessel elsewhere.

This anchor be not a feeling, but a person — Son of Skipper, Jesus — who has sailed ahead of us into heaven and prepared a berth for us in the Port of Paradise.

That be the long and short of it, mates. The anchor that keeps your life secure and destination fixed be Skipper's Son, the One who went down to the grave for you. The One who went into Sheol — the realm of the dead, the grave, the underworld, the place all the dead go — and called all bound with the chains of death to come out and rise with Him (Ephesians 4:8–9, 1 Peter 3:18–19).

Here be your charge: receive Christ Jesus as Lord and live your lives in him, anchored and built up in him, strengthened in the faith (Colossians 2:6–7).

Rooted. Built up. Strengthened. These be the commission of every soul — make your vessel properly fitted for the open sea. Then, when squalls hit and tides turn, whether in port or on passage, we have a firm anchor to keep us safe. Rode and chain in port. Sea anchor when in peril.

The Dance of the Danforth

Some years ago, an old sea dog coined a saying that has been passed down to crew and lubbers alike: *The voyage is never over until the anchor is set.*

Set. Fixed. To have a view and attitude toward the established peace and cessation of endless sailing. When the anchor be set, rest comes for the crew.

Many be the time when a vessel sails into harbor, its captain and crew confident that the perils of the sea have passed, only to discover that the bottom be hard, choked with grass, or otherwise unable to hold the flukes of an anchor. Around and around the vessel tacks, performing what sailors call the "dance of the Danforth." Each revolution, every additional attempt to get the anchor set, only finds its flukes skating across the bottom, refusing to grab hold and sink in. And until the crew sets anchor, rest remains elusive.

This be precisely the message Paul gave to the church in Colossae. Fix your mind and heart on things above, in the port of Paradise, where long life reigns.

A vessel adrift be carried along by currents, wind, and sometimes a mutinous crew. The captain, though present, be not fully in charge. External elements exert control over the vessel. And slowly, unless they can set the anchor or set the sails to gain steerage, the ship ends up on the rocks. And as sure as fate, those with the right anchor will no longer be tossed back and forth by the waves, and blown here and there by every wind that pipes up (Ephesians 4:14).

Three sheets to the wind... that be Paul's picture of a scurvy dog without an anchor. Not wicked, not rebellious. Simply unmoored and carried by whatever current be running.

Set Your Anchor Deep

When an anchor be properly set, the crew can sleep, go ashore, and relax. The anchor does its work silently, invisibly, beneath the surface. And here be what most sailors learn only after hard experience: the longer an anchor sets, the deeper the flukes go. What be placed with effort becomes, over time, immovable. Only with great deliberate force can a well-set anchor be broken free. When — through faith — Christ Jesus dwells in your hearts, ye be anchored in Skipper's love (Ephesians 3:17). And once we be in His love, we be set for life. He be your rock-solid anchor. In Him, ye will not be shaken (Psalm 62:5–6).

Drake faced storms and survived each one until he didn't. But when the Son be our anchor, nothing be able to separate us from the love of Skipper (Romans 8:38–

39). And His love be shared with us in an abundance of blessings.

The Material Blessings of Being in Christ

Skipper provides food and clothing for those who seek His kingdom first, promising that all these things be added unto you. In Him, there be no need for anxious striving over what ye shall eat or wear. He opens His hand and supplies all your needs according to His riches in the Son, not according to the poverty of your circumstances.

He gives health to your body and nourishment to your bones. He heals the brokenhearted and binds up their wounds. By the flogging and beating the Son suffered on His way to the cross, ye were healed — past tense, already done, already purchased in His pummeling. Skipper sent His word and healed you. He has delivered ye from destruction and decay in the grave. He forgives all your iniquities and heals all your diseases, and crowns ye with lovingkindness and tender mercies. He satisfies your belly with good grub. He renews your body so ye can soar like an eagle.

He gives wealth and the power to earn income. His ability to produce abundance be itself a reason we no longer need to go about pirating. Why steal when we can earn a good wage doing the thing we love? The blessings of Skipper make us rich and fill us with joy. A good man leaves an inheritance for his children and his children's children. In Christ we be Skipper's children, and He takes pleasure in our prosperity. He gives seed to the sower and bread for food, and will multiply your seed for sowing and increase the harvest of your righteousness. Ye will be enriched in every way to be generous in every way.

To those who find wisdom, He gives long life, and — with peace — adds to your days. He keeps ye safe in your going out and your coming in. He watches over you, so no evil shall land on deck, nor any plague come near your bunk. He gives His angels charge over ye to keep ye in all your ways.

He restores what the enemy has plundered, pillaged, and stolen. He gives back the years the mold and weevils have ruined. He turns mourning into a jolly jig, replaces your sackcloth with regal robes, and fills your mug with the spirit of gladness. He makes even your enemies plead for peace with you. He causes ye to triumph in every port, in every encounter.

These be not promises for another life — they be the provision of this age. Not guaranteed by personal perfection, but secured by the covenant of the Son, who became poor so that ye might become rich.

Remain in Him

With all these blessings — with such a sure anchor and hope for a better future today, good living for tomorrow, and life forever — why not strike your colours and surrender to

Jesus? Why not sign on with Him and ask Him to remain in ye and ye in Him? Apart from Him, ye can do nothing; ye may lay to that. (John 15:4)

Drake sailed under his own colours his whole life. And like all who go their own way, he lost everything — booty, crew, fame, power, prestige, and life itself. A day of dead reckoning awaits all who refuse to set their anchor in Skipper's Port of Paradise.

Hop aboard, mate. Sail with Jesus and enjoy the good life today, tomorrow, and forever.

Pirate Fact: The Master Gunner be responsible for the ship's guns and ammunition. This includes sifting the powder to keep it dry, preventing it from separating, ensuring the cannons and ordnance be kept free of rust, and that all weapons be in good repair. A knowledgeable Gunner be essential to the crew's safety and the vessel's fighting power. A loose cannon — one that breaks free of its lashings in a storm — be one of the most dangerous threats aboard any ship. Keep your weapons secured. Keep your soul anchored. Both demand the same discipline. The loose cannon and the unanchored soul have, historically, caused similar levels of damage to everyone nearby.

What Comes With Your Commission to Sail With Jesus

When ye sign on with Jesus, ye be not signing on for a life of scraping barnacles and making do. Skipper be not a stingy shipowner who works his crew to the bone and keeps the treasure locked below. He be extravagant. He be generous beyond measure. And He has put His promises in writing, so no mate can claim he weren't told what was in the contract.

Here be what the Articles say.

Provision. Skipper promises food, clothing, and all things necessary for the voyage — not as a reward for striving, but as the natural consequence of seeking His kingdom first. He opens His hand and satisfies the desire of every living thing. He supplies all your needs — not some, not most — *all* — according to His riches in glory. Not according to the poverty of your circumstances. According to *His* hold, which never runs empty. (Matthew 6:31–33, Psalm 145:16, Philippians 4:19)

Health. The Son went to the flogging post before He went to the cross. Every stripe laid on His back were laid there for a reason. Isaiah said it plainly. Peter confirmed it. By His wounds ye be healed — past tense, already purchased, already paid in full before ye ever clapped eyes on the bill. Skipper sent His word and healed them. He heals all your diseases. He redeems ye from destruction. He renews your strength until ye be soaring like an eagle off a following wind. He gives health to your body and nourishment to your bones. And when your heart be broken clean in two, He binds up the wounds. (Proverbs 3:7–8, Psalm 147:3, Isaiah 53:5, 1 Peter 2:24, Psalm 107:20, Psalm 103:3–5)

Wealth. Skipper gives ye the power to produce wealth — not as a boast, but as a confirmation of His covenant. The blessing of the Lord makes rich and adds no sorrow with it. No hidden cost. No fine print. No morning after. A good man — a man anchored in Christ — leaves an inheritance not just for his children, but for his children's children. Skipper takes pleasure in the prosperity of His crew. He multiplies your seed for sowing and increases the harvest of your righteousness, enriching ye in every way so ye can be generous in every way. The Son Himself became poor so that ye might become rich. (Deuteronomy 8:18, Proverbs 10:22, Proverbs 13:22, Psalm 35:27, 2 Corinthians 9:10–11, 2 Corinthians 8:9)

Long Life. Wisdom holds long life in her right hand. Skipper satisfies ye with length of days and shows ye His salvation. He keeps your going out and your coming in — from this day forth and forevermore. Not just on fair days. Not just in calm waters. Forevermore. (Proverbs 3:16, Psalm 91:16, Psalm 121:8)

Protection. No evil shall land on deck. No plague shall come near your bunk. He gives His angels charge over ye to keep ye in all your ways. Aye — angels. Not a single deckhand, not a watch-keeper nodding off at the rail — angels, assigned to ye, working the night watch while ye sleep. (Psalm 91:10–11)

Restoration. Whatever the enemy has stolen, plundered, or pillaged, Skipper restores. The years the mold and weevils have eaten, He gives back. He turns mourning into a jolly jig and replaces your sackcloth with regal robes. He makes even your enemies come to terms of peace with ye. He causes ye to triumph in every port, in every engagement, in every place ye set foot. (Joel 2:25, Psalm 30:11, Proverbs 16:7, 2 Corinthians 2:14)

These be not the promises of a desperate recruiter trying to fill out a crew before the tide turns. These be the sworn Articles of a Skipper who has never broken His word, never lost a vessel He captained, and never once failed to bring His crew home.

The Articles be signed. The commission be yours.

All that remains be for ye to take the helm.

Fair Warning From Skipper

Yes, sailing with Jesus be the richest life available to any soul on earth. But it be not without its hard weather.

The Son made no secret of this. He told His crew plainly: the world will hate ye on account of His name. Not might. *Will.* Those who sailed closest to Him were flogged, imprisoned, run through with swords, and fed to lions — not because they did something wrong, but because they stood right by His side. Suffering for his name will come. Ye may lay to that.

Ye will be asked to take up your cross and follow Him. That be not a metaphor for a difficult Tuesday. It be the risk that any day, ye will be called to die for His name and word. The cross be real and the weight of it be real.

But here be what Drake never knew and what every mate in this fleet must hold fast to: ye do not carry it alone. The Son said, "Come to me, all ye who are weary and burdened, and I will give you rest. Take my yoke upon you." A yoke be built for two. When ye be yoked with Christ Jesus, He be pulling alongside ye — and that cross ye bear, He helps carry. He carried His, and then got a wee bit of help. He does the same for His crew.

The cross be yours to carry. But the weight be His to share.

Ye may lose homes, family, and friends who want no part of the voyage ye be on. The Son made no pretense about this. He said so plainly that what ye lose for His sake ye will receive back in spades: houses, brothers, sisters, mothers, children, and lands, a hundred times over, with eternal life thrown in for good measure. Skipper does not ask ye to sail at a loss. The cross be real and the weight be real — but the port He be taking ye to makes every hard league of the passage worth every stroke of the oar. The Skipper be faithful through it all.

Always was.

Always will be.

www.ingramcontent.com/pod-product-compliance
Lightning Source LLC
Chambersburg PA
CBHW031350230926
51848CB00002B/468
9781965649251